MUSICAL INSTRUMENTS OF NORTH INDIA: EIGHTEENTH CENTURY PORTRAITS BY BALTAZARD SOLVYNS

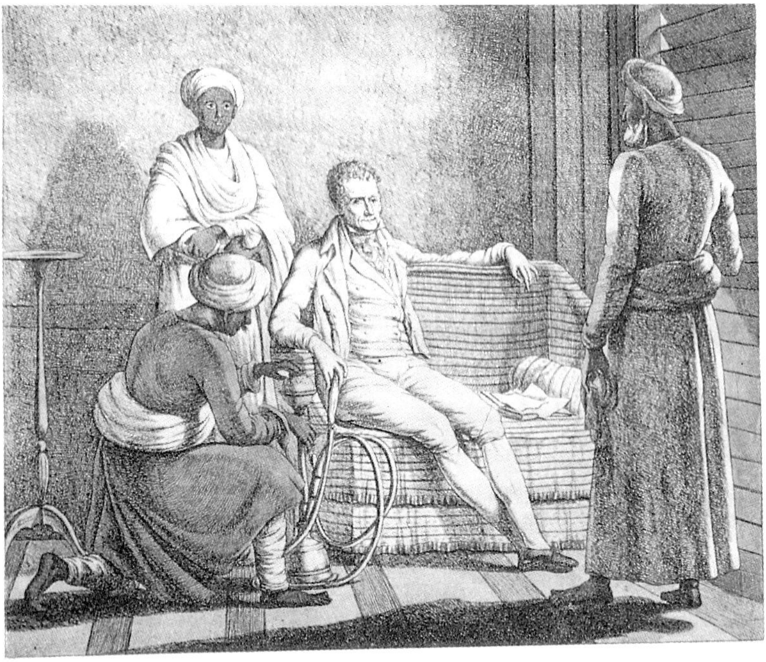

F. Baltazard Solvyns in Calcutta
Self-Portrait, *Les Hindoûs,* Vol. IV, 1812

Musical Instruments of North India

Eighteenth Century Portraits by Baltazard Solvyns

ROBERT L. HARDGRAVE, JR.
STEPHEN M. SLAWEK

MANOHAR
1997

First published 1997

ISBN 81-7304-165-2

Published by
Ajay Kumar Jain for
Manohar Publishers & Distributors
2/6 Ansari Road, Daryaganj
New Delhi 110 002

Lasertypeset by
A J Software Publishing Co. Pvt. Ltd.
305 Durga Chambers
1333 D.B. Gupta Road
Karol Bagh, New Delhi 110 005

Printed at
Rajkamal Electric Press
B 35/9 G T Karnal Road Indl Area
Delhi 110033

Contents

Acknowledgments

To colleagues who assisted us in pursuit of what often seemed to be elusive words and images, we wish to express our thanks: Deben Bhattacharya, Paris; Joep Bor, Rotterdam; Shubha Chaudhuri, New Delhi; R. P. Gupta, Calcutta; Daniel Neuman, Los Angeles; Pran Nevile, New Delhi; and Anita Slawek, Austin. And we are grateful to Aditi Sen, Calcutta, and Sagaree Sen Gupta, Austin, for their assistance in Bengali transliteration.

Thanks go as well to the American Institute of Indian Studies and to the University Research Institute of the University of Texas at Austin for support in the larger Solvyns project.

The University of Texas at Austin
December 1995

ROBERT L. HARDGRAVE, JR.
STEPHEN M. SLAWEK

Introduction

To the European in India in the eighteenth century, Indian music was surely strange and exotic, and to many it was little more than noise, cacophonous and irritating. Captain Donald Campbell, in his *Journey Over Land to India* (1781-1784), described it as "inelegant, harsh and dissonant".[1] Pierre Sonnerat, in the account of his voyage, wrote of Indian musical instruments, "That which makes the greatest noise is to them the most harmonious and pleasing."[2] The Abbé J. A. Dubois, an astute observer of India in the late eighteenth and early nineteenth century, wrote that "what they [the Hindus] like is plenty of noise and plenty of shrill piercing sounds";[3] and Walter Hamilton, writing in 1820, described Indian music as "disagreeable" and "insufferable".[4] J. R. Martin, in 1837, complained from Calcutta, "It is impossible to speak of Bengalee music with any feeling short of disgust, or to compare it to any thing but the noise made by cows in distress, with an admixture of the caterwauling of a feline congregation and the occasional scream of a affrighted elephant."[5] But for many officers, merchants, and administrators of the British East India Company who had been influenced by the tastes and habits of the Indian gentry and for those "adventurers" who had settled into Indian life, "country musick" might be heard with pleasure. The nautch especially enjoyed a vogue among Europeans in India. Percival Spear notes that "it became the recognized form of entertainment for an Indian merchant to provide for his Indian guests", and the tradition continued into the nineteenth century long after the European taste for nautch had disappeared.[6]

Indian music for most Europeans was, at best, a diversion, but for the members of the Asiatic Society in Calcutta, it was a matter of scholarly inquiry. Sir William Jones, the great Orientalist and doyen of the Society, wrote "On the Musical Modes of the Hindus", published in 1792 in the third volume of *Asiatick Researches.*[7] Another scholar-administrator in service of the East India Company, Francis Fowke, provided a detailed description of the bīn, or vīṇā, with an engraving depicting the instrument.[8] But it is to a Flemish artist, François Baltazard Solvyns, that we owe the first systematic portrayal of Indian musical instruments and the manner in which they were played.[9]

Born in Antwerp in 1760, Solvyns[10] had pursued a career principally as a marine painter until political unrest in Europe and his own insecure position led him to seek his fortune in India. India in the late eighteenth century had attracted a number of British artists who found a ready market for their works among the Europeans of Calcutta and Madras and in the courts of the Indian princes. Thomas Hodges, and later Thomas and William Daniell, sold landscapes, but the most handsome profits were to be made in portraiture, and here such painters as Tilly Kettle, Thomas Hickey, and John Zoffany enjoyed the patronage of nabobs and nawabs alike.[11]

Solvyns was adept at neither landscape nor portraiture, and upon his arrival in Calcutta in 1791, he became something of a journeyman artist. He provided decoration for celebrations and balls, cleaned and restored paintings, and offered instruction in oils, watercolor, and chalk. The decoration of coaches and palanquins apparently provided Solvyns his steadiest income, but hardly the success and sense of accomplishment he clearly sought. In 1794, inspired by Sir William Jones, Solvyns announced his plan to prepare *A Collection of Two Hundred and Fifty Coloured Etchings: Descriptive of the Manners, Customs and Dresses of the Hindoos.*

With a sufficient number of subscribers to begin, Solvyns set out to record the life of the native quarter of Calcutta, or "Blacktown", as it was then called. He approached his task as an ethnographer, drawing his subjects from life and with more concern for accuracy than aesthetics. The collection was published in Calcutta in a few copies in 1796, and then in greater numbers in 1799. Divided into twelve parts, the first section, with 66 prints, depicts "the Hindoo Casts, with their professions". Following sections portray servants, costumes, means of transportation (carts, palanquins, and boats), modes of smoking, fakirs, and festivals. Section XI contains 36 prints of musical instruments.

The project proved a financial failure. The etchings, by contemporary European standards, were rather crudely done; the forms and settings were monotonous; and the colors were of somber hue. They did not, in short, appeal to the vogue of the picturesque. But the subjects were themselves compelling, and London publisher Edward Orme brought out a pirated edition of 60 prints "after Solvyns", redrawn for appeal and colored in warm pastels. The volume, *The Costume of Indoostan* (1804, 1807), through various printings, was highly successful, but Solvyns derived no gain and suffered, as he later wrote, "abuse ... made of his name and of his works".[12]

In 1804, Solvyns left India for France, and soon after his return to Europe married Mary Ann Greenwood, daughter of an English family resident in Ghent. In Paris, drawing upon his wife's resources, Solvyns prepared new etchings and produced a folio edition of 288 plates, *Les Hindoûs,* published in Paris between 1808 and 1812 in four elephantine volumes. In his introduction, Solvyns writes that while European scholars have done much "to dispel the darkness which enveloped the geography and history of India, . . . its inhabitants alone have not yet been observed nor represented with the accuracy which is necessary to make them perfectly known. . . ." To rectify this situation, he offered to the public *Les Hindoûs,* "the result of a long and uninterrupted study of this celebrated nation".[13]

> The drawings from which are engraved the numerous plates . . . were taken by myself upon the spot. Instead of trusting to the words of others, or remaining satisfied with the knowledge contained in preceding authors, I have spared neither time, nor pains, nor expense, to see and examine with my own eyes, and to delineate every object with the most minute accuracy. . . .
>
> I admitted nothing as certain but upon the proof of my own observation, or upon such testimony as I knew to be incontrovertible. I have wholly neglected the testimony of authors who have treated these subjects before me, and have given only what I have seen, or what I have myself heard from the mouth of the natives the best informed and most capable of giving me true instructions upon the subject of my inquiries.

What I have said of the text, may also in some degree be applied to the prints themselves, in which I have purposely avoided all sort of ornament or embellishment; they are meerly representations of the objects such as they appeared to my view. . . .[14]

Drawings . . . of their several musical instruments have been published, but in a very imperfect manner; in the first place, they do no more than represent the instrument, without giving an idea of the manner in which it is played, which is not easy to conceive without having it under the eye: the figures too are so small, that it is not possible to guess the parts of which they are composed, and still less to make one of them. The manner in which I have drawn these different instruments in my collection is not, if I am not mistaken, liable to any of these objections.[15]

In the text accompanying the plates of the Paris edition, Solvyns describes the musicians as largely from the lower castes—scavengers, leather workers, palanquin carriers—and often the disreputable and dissolute among them, whom he terms *Loutchias* and *Pariahs.* Solvyns identifies a few instruments, notably string (such as the bīn or vīṇā), with brahmins, but drums, most wind instruments, and many stringed instruments are the preserve of the "untouchable" Hindu castes and of Muslims. Drums or stringed instruments with gut or skins, such as the sāraṅgī (Pl. 9), are a source of ritual pollution. And the tradition—to which Solvyns alludes in his discussion of the flute (bā̃śi, Pl. 37)—is that the high castes are prohibited from playing wind instruments because of, as Abbé Dubois explains, "the defilement which the players contact by putting such instruments in their mouths after they have been touched by saliva . . . . There is by no means the same feeling with regard to stringed instruments. In fact, you may often hear Brahmins singing and accompanying themselves on a sort of lute which is known by the name *vina*. . . . It has always been a favourite amongst the better classes."[16] Sir William Jones noted that in India music is "known and practiced . . . not by mercenary performers only, but even by *Mussalmans* and *Hindoos* of eminent rank and learning".[17]

Solvyns emphasizes that his discourse is on the Hindus, as distinct from Muslims, for whom he expresses distain, and in the text on musical instruments, he seeks, as elsewhere, to distinguish that which is *Hindu* from contaminating Muslim influences.[18] That was surely not easy in late eighteenth century Bengali society, especially among professional musicians. Persian, the court language of the Mughals, was still the language of administration—as it remained in British India until 1835. Upper class Hindus—or at least those who sought jobs or influence in government, whether under the Mughals or the British—were educated in Persian, Hindustani (Urdu), and often Arabic, in addition to Sanskrit and their native Bengali. Many cultivated Muslim culture. Naba Krishna (Nobkissen), Clive's Persian translator and political adviser, was a Hindu. Ram Mohan Roy (1772-1833) mastered Persian and Arabic before he learned English. Hindu musicians of the Hindustani tradition, as distinct from the Bengali folk idiom, surely knew Persian and Urdu and then, as today, probably wore Muslim costume.

In the Preliminary Discourse for *Les Hindoûs,* Solvyns writes that "Music is very generally cultivated among the Hindoos, especially as it is subservient to dancing, one of their favourite diversions", and he notes that "we may form a judgment of the character of this art in Hindoostan" from publications by Sir William Jones, William Hamilton Bird, and Baron d'Alberg.[19] Solvyns rejects the use of secondary sources in his descriptions of the instruments he portrays, relying solely, he tells us, on his own observation, but in his introduction, Solvyns draws upon Jones's "On Musical Modes of the Hindus".[20] "What may be collected from that work," Solvyns writes,

> is, that the Hindoos believe their music to be a present of the divinity, and, with the rest of the fine arts, of celestial origin. That part of their mythology which concerns music is justly represented by Sir William Jones as a delightful and graceful allegory: Brahma himself bestowed music upon mankind, through the mediation of his active power, called the divinity who presides over language, and whose son *Nereda* [Narada] invented the *Vina,* the finest instrument of their ancient music. There are four musical systems, which have a sensible relation to the four seasons of the year, each of which has its analogous mode. The melancholy is well adapted to the cold and gloomy season of the latter end of autumn; one more gay and lively suits the season where nature seems to revive; the heats of summer require more languid tones; the autumn, in fine, has a brilliant mode congenial to the feelings, where the rains give new life to the drooping vegetation, and create a sort of second spring.

Each of these modes in the Hindoo music is a celestial spirit, a grand Harwa [*rāga*]; and each of these aerial musicians is allied or married to five nymphs or Rageni [*rāgiṇī*], and the father of eight little genii. From the marriage of these grand *Harwas* proceeds what mortals call harmony; and melody is nothing more than the succession of generations issuing from these alliances. Music then in their sacred writings is but the figurative system of accords between celestial beings, and of the harmonic alliance between the aerial spirits called *Tones.*

Sir William Jones tells us, that he had given himself much useless trouble to discover some piece of ancient music which might have been preserved, as he supposed among the Brahmins. We have to regret with this learned gentleman, that nothing remains except the theory of their music, and that we can form but a very imperfect judgment of the effect of their musical compositions, to which they themselves attribute the power of raising and of calming the human passions, of enchanting the most savage animals and subduing their ferocity. In music, especially combined with dancing and singing, they suppose these supernatural powers: Among the Hindoos these three arts were formerly closely connected; it is remarkable that the metre of their poetry is always in conformity with the sentiment which it wishes to inspire, and that it varies like music with the nature of the subject. This attention of their poets gave the greatest effect to their words when they were sung and accompanied by music and pantomine perfectly adapted to them. But there is nothing like regularity or systematic arrangment in the actual music of the Hindoos. My work gives only a description of their instruments; but it is accompanied with remarks which will, I believe, be sufficient to give an idea of what their music is at present, and must have been for ages past: for . . . it may be seen that changes do not take place in India with as much facility as in the nations of Europe where the arts are always influenced by the genius of the times.[21]

Solvyns's portrayal of the Hindus has over two centuries received little recognition in scholarly literature on Indian culture and society, with few references even in historical and ethnographic works on Bengal. The Dutch ethnomusicologist Jaap Kunst, in a 1945 article, might be said to have "discovered" the Solvyns etchings depicting musical instruments,[22] and Mantle Hood, in 1963, brought Solvyns again to light with a discussion of his portrayal of instruments. "Historically," Hood writes, "*Les Hindous* is especially valuable for the fine engravings . . . showing in many instances the playing positions of a number of Indian instruments no longer in use today. Without this reference the actual method of playing many instruments would be largely speculative."[23] And the Dutch ethnomusicologist Joep Bor, in "The Voice of the Sarangi: An Illustrated History of Bowing in India", refers extensively to Solvyns and reproduces five Solvyns etchings.[24] In the journal *Asian Music*, we published "Instruments and Music Culture in Eighteenth Century India: The Solvyns Portraits",[25] for the first time bringing Solvyns's important etchings to a wider audience. The present volume extends and revises that earlier work.

A Note on the Solvyns Plates and Text and on the Annotations

Throughout *Les Hindoûs*, Solvyns refers to music and instruments in association with festivals and in relation to particular castes or occupations, and he includes instruments in etchings of various festivals and of the nauch. Thirty-five plates in *Les Hindoûs*, Volume II, depict musical instruments, each identified in Solvyns's transliteration from Bengali, with accompanying French and English text. The organization of the Paris edition is different from that of the earlier Calcutta collection, and to fit the new format, Solvyns omitted one of the prints—the "Burung"—included among the earlier etchings of musical instruments. For *Musical Instruments of North India*, we reproduce the 35 plates of the Paris edition as well as "Burung" from the Calcutta edition. In addition to the instruments, we include from the Paris edition Solvyns's portrayal of the "Ramjanny", dancing girl, and, in large format, the Nautch.[26] The prints are organized and numbered in the order of the Paris edition, with "Burung" at the end. In our annotations, references to specific Solvyns etchings not included in this book are by volume/section/number in the Paris edition; thus, Kān, a Hindu singer, is identified as I.11.3.

The English text accompanying the portraits of the musical instruments of *Les Hindoûs* has been reproduced here as it appears in the original. The annotations clarify and elaborate Solvyns's text while directing the reader to relevant literature.[27] The single most comprehensive source for information on Indian instruments is *The New Grove Dictionary of Musical Instruments* (NGMI), and it is needless for us to duplicate what is available there and in other recent sources on Indian musical instruments.

There is considerable regional variation in the names of instruments, and each may be variously transliterated. For instrument names, we use the Roman transliteration following NGMI or, for distinct Bengali forms, that closest to Solvyns's term. When possible, our first citation to the instrument portrayed is to the volume and page number of NGMI where it is discussed. Also provided are the transliterations as given in NGMI, variant terms and names of related instruments. Footnotes for the text and annotations for the Solvyns portraits use shortened references to the sources cited, referring the reader to the bibliography.

For each plate, we include the descriptive text from Solvyns's *A Catalogue of 250 Coloured Etchings; Descriptive of the Manners, Customs, Characters, Dress, and Religious Ceremonies of the Hindoos,* published in Calcutta in 1799 to accompany the collection of etchings,[28] as well as Solvyns's more detailed text for the Paris edition, *Les Hindoûs.*

We also note those plates in the Orme pirated edition. Of the 60 plates in *The Costume of Indoostan,* 16 depict musical instruments (28; 46-60). Each depicts Solvyns's central figure, sometimes with slight variation in form, and leaves out the background, save for the depiction of the śaṅkh and ghaṇṭā (Pl. 46), where the artist modifies and simplifies the background in portraying a woman at pūjā. The text accompanying each plate in the Orme edition provides little more than the Solvyns description from the 1799 *Catalogue,* sometimes incorporating Solvyns's account of a festival or caste group from another *Catalogue* entry. The notable exception is the Orme text to the plate (No. 50) depicting the pinãk. Titled, "Pennauck, or Been", the two instruments are confused, and the Orme text describes not a pinãk, but a bīn—lifting the description, without acknowledgment, from an article in *Asiatick Researches.*

The plates from the Calcutta edition depicting musicial instruments will be included in Robert L. Hardgrave, Jr., *A Portrait of the Hindus: Baltazard Solvyns in Calcutta, 1791-1804,* a forthcoming volume that will reproduce the complete collection of the Solvyns etchings, with annotations and introductory chapters on the artist's life and work and on the Calcutta of his times.

NOTES

1 3: 124, quoted in Percival Spear, *The Nabobs: A Study of the Social Life of the English in Eighteenth Century India* (London: Oxford University Press, 1963), 34.

2 *A Voyage of the East-Indies and China*, tr. from the French (Calcutta; Stuart and Cooper, 1788), 2: 124.

3 *Hindu Manners, Customs and Ceremonies*, 3rd ed. (Oxford: Clarendon Press, 1959 [1816]), 64.

4 *A Description of Hindoostan* (Delhi: Oriental Publishers, 1971 [1820]), 1: 103.

5 James Ranald Martin, *Notes on the Medical Topography of Calcutta* (Calcutta: Bengal Military Orphen Press, 1837), 51-52.

6 Spear, 35. From the end of the eighteenth century, as social contact between Indians and Europeans became both less frequent and less intimate, "the English taste [for nautch] gradually changed from a slightly guilty appreciation or naive enjoyment to frank incomprehension, boredom and finally disgust". Spear, 35. Dennis Kencaid, in *British Social Life in India, 1608-1937* (London: George Routledge & Sons, 1938), also notes this change in European attitudes in the late eighteenth century, as Indian music, once enjoyed, becomes "horrid screeching" and "disgusting caterwauling". p. 105.

7 The article, originally written in 1784, was published in an expanded version in *Asiatick Researches* (London: 1807 [1792]), 3: 55-87. Reprinted in Sourindro Mohun Tagore, ed., *Hindu Music From Various Authors*, Chowkhamba Sanskrit Studies, No. 49 (Varanasi: Chowkhamba Sanskrit Series Office, 1965 [1882]), 125-60. In an earlier article, "On the Gods of *Greece, Italy,* and *India*", *Asiatick Researches,* (London: 1806 [1788]), 1: 264-65, Jones briefly discusses Indian music and, in a plate, includes a copy of an Indian miniature painting depicting the god Narada with the bīn (vīṇā), the instrument, according to tradition, he invented.

8 "On the *Veena,* or *Indian* Lyre", An Extract of a Letter from Francis Fowke, Esq. to the President, *Asiatick Researches* (London: 1806 [1788]), 1: 295-99. Reprinted in Tagore, 191-97. The engraving in the Fowke article is reproduced in the commentary on the Bīn (Pl. 6).

9 Solvyns's South Indian counterpart in the 1790s was Charles Gold, whose work was produced in 50 colored plates, half of which present figures in costume with accompanying descriptive text.

Plate 22 depicts musical instruments, numbered and identified. *Oriental Drawings, Sketched Between 1791 and 1798* (London: G. & W. Nicoll, 1806).

10 Solvyns used his middle name, Baltazard, rather than François. On Solvyns, see Robert L. Hardgrave, Jr. "A Portrait of Black Town: Baltazard Solvyns in Calcutta, 1791-1804", in *Changing Visions, Lasting Images: Calcutta Through 300 Years,* ed. Pratapaditya Pal (Bombay: Marg, 1990), 31-46; Mildred Archer and W. G. Archer, "Francois Baltazard Solvyns: Early Painter of Calcutta Life", in *Science, Philosophy and Culture: Essays Presented in Honour of Humayun Kabir's Sixty-Second Birthday,* eds. Frank Moraes *et al.* (Bombay: Asia Publishing House, 1968), 1-10; and Mildred Archer, "Baltazard Solvyns and the Indian Picturesque", *The Connoisseur,* 170 (January 1969): 12-18.

11 See Mildred Archer, *India and British Portraiture, 1770-1825* (London: Sotheby Parke Bernet, 1979).

12 *Les Hindoûs* (Paris: Chez L'Auteur, 1808), 1: 29.

13 Ibid., 1: 20-21.

14 Ibid., 1: 21.

15 Ibid., 1: 26-27.

16 Dubois, 64-65.

17 Jones, "On the Musical Modes of the Hindus", 62, in Tagore, 133.

18 Solvyns was also concerned about European influence. In expressing admiration for the Hindu, Solvyns writes, "Simplicity and temperance are virtues common to the whole race, and are remarked in every part of Hindoostan which has escaped the fatal influence of European manners." *Les Hindoûs,* 1: 22.

19 Ibid., 1: 26. See Bird, *The Oriental Miscellany: Being a Collection of the Most Favourite Airs of Hindoostan, Compiled and Adapted for the Harpsicord, &c.* (Calcutta: Joph. Cooper, 1789), and Baron Johan Friedrich Hugo von d'Alberg (Dalberg), *Ueber die Musik der Indier Eine Ubhandlung des Sir William Jones* (Erfurt: Beyer und Maring, 1802). The later is a German translation of Jones's "On the Musical Modes of the Hindus", and includes plates depicting musical instruments. For a detailed discussion of early European accounts of Indian music, see Joep Bor, "The Rise of Ethnomusicology: Sources on Indian Music *c.* 1780-*c.* 1890", *Yearbook for Traditional Music,* 20 (1988): 51-73.

20 See fn. 7.

21 *Les Hindoûs,* 2: 15-16.

22 "Een Vergeten Musicologische Bron: De Instrumentafbeeldingen in 'Les Hindous' Van F. Baltazard Solvyns", *Cultureel Indië* (Leiden) 7 (1945): 197-200.

23 "Music, the Unknown", in *Musicology*, eds, Frank Harrison *et al.* (Englewood Cliffs, NJ: Prentice-Hall, 1963), 220. Hood reproduces Solvyns's plates for the Soorna and the nautch.

24 *National Centre for the Performing Arts, Quarterly Journal* (Bombay), 15-16 (1986-87): 1-183. Bor also discusses Solvyns in "The Rise of Ethnomusicology".

25 20 (Fall/Winter 1988-89): 1-92.

26 The reproductions for this volume are of Solvyns etchings in the collection of Robert L. Hardgrave, Jr.

27 There are a vast number of musical instruments in India, but a useful visual overview may be found in the chapter on "Indian Musical Instruments", with 200 line drawings, in Vishnudass Shirali, *Sargam: An Introduction to Indian Music* (New Delhi: Abhinav/Marg, 1977). Many instruments from Bengal are illustrated with photographs in A. M. Meerwarth, *A Guide to the Collection of Musical Instruments Exhibited in the Ethnographic Galley of the Indian Museum, Calcutta* (Calcutta: Zoological Survey of India, 1917).

28 Published in quarto (Calcutta: Mirror Press, 1799), the *Catalogue* contains brief descriptions of the etchings, usually no more than a few words or a paragraph at most.

1. Nautch

Calcutta: Plate before Section IV. A Nautch or Hindostany Dance.
Paris: II.2.1. Nautch Hindoo Dance

It is to be observed that the dance represented in this plate has nothing in common with that which is performed all over India, by women known by the name of *Bayaderes, Baladeres* or *Bays;* a description of which is found in the works of many travellers. As this amusement is foreign to the true Hindoos, and known only among the other Indians, the Mussulmen, Portuguese, etc., it could not form a part of this collection. But here is a short description of an original Hindoo dance called *Nautch.*

This dance is generally executed by three female dancers or *Ramjannys,* who are courtesans as well as the *Bayaderes.* It is opened by a single dancer, who is joined successively by the two others in a great variety of motions, and of very graceful and often very lascivious attitudes. An European accustomed to look upon the dances of his own country as the perfection of the art, would be surprised to see the languid ease, the natural grace, the voluptuous suppleness, displayed in every movement of the accomplished *Ramjanny.* We must not wonder if this beautiful dance is but little known even to those who have resided some time in India; it is of late seldom performed by Hindoos, and is more in vogue among the Mussulmen and in the north of Hindoostan than in the south. It is besides now frequently danced by the *Bayaderes* who have corrupted it by so much obscene actions and attitudes, that its original character is no longer to be known. What has caused this diversion to degenerate still more, is it being sometimes danced by *Hidgras* [*hijṛā*] (hermaphrodites), or by dissolute young men who accompany all their motions with the most libidinous and immoral songs.

NAUTCH. Paris II.2.1.

The instruments to which the *Ramjannys* dance the *Nautch* are the *been* [*bīn*], the *sitar* and others with cords [strings]; whereas the Mussulmen use only the *sarinda,* the *tubla* [*tablā*] and the *d'hola* [*ḍhol*], each of which shall have its particular description in the course of the present volume.

Formerly the princes and grandees of the country, kept troops of dancing girls in their pay, who attended them everywhere as a part of their suite. This practice has now totally ceased. It is only at feasts that these women, who are generally prostitutes, are hired for money, so that no great beauty nor freshness can be expected in these miserable victims of debauchery.

At great festivals, such as the marriage of some rich person, or a *poojah* [*pūjā*] or *durgah* [Durgā Pūjā], twenty or thirty of these dancing girls, and from thirty to fifty musicians are hired. The *Ramjannys* move in groups three by three, and perform the *Nautch* in every part of their vast halls, often varying the spot, and following the company to the sound of the instruments.

I shall have occasion to describe the dress of these dancers in this number.

Commentary

The nautch (*nāc* in Bengali, from the Sanskrit *nṛtya,* "to dance") was a form of entertainment by "dancing girls" that became popular among affluent Hindus in Bengal, especially in celebration of Durgā Pūjā, in the late eighteenth and early nineteenth centuries. Its character was similar to katthak, the dance tradition associated with Muslim courtesans of North India.

In early accounts of life and travels in India, Europeans almost invariably included a description of the nautch,[1] and both professional and amateur artists—Tilly Kettle, Thomas Hickey, Thomas Daniell, and Charles D'Oyly, for example—portrayed the nautch in all its sensuous grace.[2] Solvyns was the first European to depict the nautch in a print, and in visual representations of Indian life in publications that followed, as well as in the many paintings produced for Europeans by the Indian Company School artists, the nautch continued to fascinate well into the nineteenth century.[3] By the 1830s, however, Europeans, once "addicted" to the nautch, were less inclined to attend such functions, and the nautch as an after-supper entertainment in European households, the fashion when few European women graced Calcutta society, gave way to the increasingly frequent round of both private and public balls.[4]

A nautch might be attended by as many as seven or eight hundred people, and wealthy Hindus in Calcutta frequently invited Europeans—usually by printed invitation. "When a black man has a mind to compliment a European," Mrs. Nathaniel Kindersley wrote in 1767, "he treats him to a nautch."[5]

Most Europeans were captivated by the nautch, but some were clearly bored, as was the Rev. William Tennant in 1797: "Though the Notches are intended to do honor to some deity, who presides over the festival; yet they seem of all institutions the least calculated to excite religious ideas. Part of the ceremony consists of listening to the music of the singing girls, who drawl out their monotonous ditties with a nonchalance and dulness, which can only be equalled by the sluggish dance, and the inanimate gestures with which they are accomplished. Of all entertainments, an Hindostanee Notch is the most insipid. . . . Yet such invitations are given from politeness, it is proper that they should be accepted, with at least an appearance of satisfaction."[6]

Mrs. Kindersley, in 1767, found the nautch "very delightful", but noted the dancers' "languishing glances, wanton smiles, and attitudes" were "not quite consistent with decency. . . ."[7] Other European accounts, especially those later into the nineteenth century, occasionally described the nautch as "indecent", some even expressed disgust,[8] but Mrs. Reginald Heber, wife of the Bishop of Calcutta, wrote in her diary of the nautch girls that she "never saw public dancing in England so free from every thing approaching to indecency. Their dress was modesty itself, but their faces, feet, and hands exposed to view."[9]

Although the nautch was usually associated with religious festivals, it was sometimes staged specifically for European guests. William Hickey's *Bengal Gazette*, August 18-25, 1781, provides an account of "a nautch and magnificent entertainment" given by Raja Nobkissen (Nabakrishna), banian to the East Indian Company and credited with introducing the nautch into Calcutta society.[10] That the nautch often took the character of a variety show is evident in various descriptions of not only dancers, but "bands of music, both European and native, tumblers, jugglers, actors, and pantomimes. . . ." All of this was then followed by "a sumptuous supper, where champagne circulated like water, and the richest ices were melted in the most costly liquors". But of such suppers, the Hindus did not partake.[11]

The Raja Rajkissen, described as "an opulent and respectable Hindoo", continued the tradition of his father Raja Nobkissen, hosting nautches over three nights during Durgā Pūjā. Maria Graham, an astute and sympathetic observer and perhaps the first woman Orientalist, provides a detailed account of the nautch—her first—on the occasion of Durgā Pūjā, in October 1810, at the home of Rajkissen. Mrs. Graham describes the house—in Sobhabazar, off Chitpur Road, in North Calcutta—as "fine", and writes,

> The room into which we were ushered was a large square court, covered in for the occasion with red cloth, to which a profusion of white artificial flowers was fastened. Three sides of the court are occupied by the dwelling-house, the walls of which are adorned by a double row of pillars in couplets, and between each couplet is a window. The fourth side is occupied by the family temple, of a very pretty architecture. . . . A flight of steps leads to the veranda of the temple, where Vishnu [more likely Durgā] sat in state, with a blaze of light before him, in magnificent chandeliers. When we entered there were some hundreds of people assembled, and there seemed to be room for as many more. The dancing was begun, but as soon as our host perceived us he led us to the most commodious seats, stationed boys behind us with round fans of red silk, with gold fringe, and then presented us with bouquets of the mogree [jasmine] and the rose, tied up with a green leaf, ornamented with silver fringe. A small gold vase being brought, the Maha Rajah, with a golden spoon, perfumed us with ottur [attar], and sprinkled us with rose-water, after which we were allowed to sit and look on. The first dancers were men [possibly *hijṛās*], whom by their dresses I took for women, though I was surprised at the assurance of their gestures, which had nothing else remarkable in them. These gave way to some Cashmerian [Kashmiri] singers, whose voices were very pleasing. They were accompanied by an old man, whose long white beard and hair, and fair skin, spoke a more northern country than Bengal. His instrument was a particularly sweet-toned guitar, which he touched with skill and taste to some of the odes of Hafiz and some Hindostanee songs. I was sorry when he finished, to make way for a kind of pantomime, in which men

personated elephants, bears, and monkeys. After this some women danced; but though they were pretty, and their motions rather graceful, I was disappointed, after hearing so much of the nautch-girls of India. One of them, while dancing in a circle, twisted a piece of striped muslin into flowers, keeping each stripe for a different coloured flower. The last amusement we staid to partake of, was the exhibition of a ventriloquist (the best I have ever heard), although the Maha Rajah pressed us to remain, saying he had different sets of dancers, enough to exhibit during the whole night. I was pleased with the attention the Rajah paid to his guests, whether Hindoos, Christians, or Mussulmans; there was not one to whom he did not speak kindly, or pay some compliment on their entrance; and he walked round the assembly repeatedly, to see that all were properly accommodated.

I am sorry I could not go to his nautch the next night, where I hear there was a masquerade, when several Portuguese and Pariahs appeared as Europeans, and imitated our dances, music, and manners.[12]

Another European visitor to the house of Rajkissen, sometime between 1811 and 1814, described the "room" where the nautch was held as "supported by twelve pillars of the Corinthian order, round which were entwined fine silk and wreaths of flowers; in the middle was spread a carpet, for the European part of the company, and on each side was ranged in rows and seats on pillows, the most respectable natives".[13]

In the great mansions of the wealthy Hindus like Rajkissen, the nautch was typically held in the courtyard at the center of the house, covered over for the occasion by a scarlet canopy, just as Maria Graham and the anonymous visitor described it. The artist William Prinsep portrays such a pillared courtyard with its canopy, with the family temple open to one side, in his watercolor, "Entertainment during the Durga puja", *c.* 1840.[14]

For these entertainments, European women joined the men, but the Hindu women remained secluded in their upper floor apartments, peering down into the courtyard through louvered blinds or latticework at the activities below. "European ladies, on the evening of the Doorga poojah, are asked to visit the female part of the family, whom they have always found apparently happy and full of curiosity."[15]

Among the entertainers at the house of Rajkissen, described by the anonymous guest, was "a beautiful girl, and very superior singer, Neekhee. . . . She was about fourteen years of age, and possessed a form and face moulded by the graces; her black eyes, full and piercing, reflected the pleasurable sensations of her heart; her mouth, around which a smile was ever playing, enclosed teeth, regular, perfect, and white as ivory; her voice was feeble; but inexpressibly sweet; and . . . I must own myself much gratified, and confess, that the twelve hundred rupees (one hundred and fifty pounds), and two pair of shawls of the same value, the price of Neekhee's attendance for three nights, was only commensurate with her singular accomplishments."[16] The celebrated Nicki (spellings vary) reigned supreme for many years. Mrs. Heber heard her—"a songstress of great reputation"—at a nautch in 1823,[17] and that same year, Fanny Parks heard her at the home of the great reformer Ramohan Roy.[18] Emma Roberts, writing in 1835, described her as "*prima donna* of the East".[19]

Solvyns distinguishes the dancers of the true nautch—*Ramjannys* [*Rāmjanī*], as he identified them—from the *Bayaderes*, who had, in his judgment, corrupted the nautch as it was most widely performed—especially as it took the form of a variety show—and as typically described by Europeans. And he deplores the degradation of the nautch by *hijṛās*, eunuchs dressed as women who sing and dance in often lewd parody. Solvyns depicts the Ramjanny (Pl. 3) and the Hijṛā (II.3.4) in a separate etchings.

Dancers were not limited to nautch performances. In his portrayal of Hindu marriage (II.6.1), Solvyns refers to chariots in the wedding procession "filled with Ramjannys (dancers) and even Hidjeras (singers), who with bands of music and other objects add to the festivity and pomp".

Dancers and musicians in Bengal came from a variety of low Hindu castes and, especially dancers, from among Muslims, although Herbert H. Risley notes that "no Hindu will have a Muhamadan musician in his house if he can possibly avoid it".[20] The Nar, or Nat, of eastern Bengal is a dancing and musician caste,[21] and a number of low castes have specific sub-castes that are musicians by occupation.

James Wise, in his ethnographic notes on predominantly Muslim East Bengal, terms the musical group accompanying the nautch "Taifa-dar",[22] and writes, "This is the musical party which attends nautch girls, who are always Muhammadans. It consists of two players on the violin (sārangī), two men who beat drums (tablā), and a player on the cymbals (manjīrā)."[23] Joep Bor, from miniature paintings and European prints, as well as from European accounts, identifies various instruments used in accompanying the nautch—the sāraṅgī, sitār, tablā, and manjīrā.[24] In portraying the nautch, Solvyns depicts a group of eight musicians playing the bīn, manjīrā, jhā̃jharī, sāraṅgī, pakhāvaj, tablā, and ḍholak.

NOTES

1 See "Some Examples of Impressions of Indian Dancing and Music", Dyson, 336-56.

2 See Nevile, "The Nautch Girl and the Sahib" and *Nautch Girls of India*. Kettle's 1772 oil painting, "Colonel Antoine Louis Henri Polier Watching a Nautch", is now lost, but a superb gouache copy was done by a Mughal artist, *c.* 1780. It depicts Polier, engineer and Orientalist, dressed in Indian clothing and reclining on cushions as he watches a nautch performed for his personal enjoyment. Welch, 88-89. Kettle also painted nautch girls *c.* 1770 and in 1772, in Archer, *India and British Portraiture*, plate 26, pp. 70-72; and plate 31, p. 79; and Thomas Hickey painted the dancers *c.* 1805, Archer, plate 126, p. 204. Thomas Daniell, from a sketch done in India, painted "The Nautch" in 1810, reproduced in Shellim, 70.

3 Among early prints depicting the nautch, the three by Mrs. S. C. Belnos, in her *Twenty-Four Plates Illustrative of Hindoo and European Manners in Bengal*, are noteworthy. Among the last prints depicting the nautch was that by the Russian artist Prince Alexis Soltykoff, in his lithographic collection, *Indian Scenes and Characters*, published in 1858, a year after the Sepoy Mutiny. It depicts European guests with their wealthy Hindu host at a nautch in the "Festival of the Goddess Durga at Calcutta", reproduced in Pal and Dehejia, plate 63, p. 72. Numerous Company School paintings depict dancing girls or nautch performances. See, for example, Archer, *Company Paintings:* 93, 156-57, 160, and 164-65. European fascination with the nautch continued into the age of photography, as seen in "Nautch Girl", *c.* 1875, in Pal and Dehejia, plate 217, p. 208.

4 Nayak, 114, 119. Charles D'Oyly portrayed "A Dancing Woman" before European men in Lucknow, plate XV, in his *European in India*.

5 *Letters . . .* , 230. Mrs. Kindersley provides one of the earliest descriptions of a nautch—and surely the earliest by a European woman—in a letter dated Ahmedabad, October 1767, pp. 229-33.

6 *Indian Recreation,* 1: 55-56. Bayly, in *Indian Society and the Making of the British Empire,* 39, describes Tennant as "supercilious" and as someone who condemned "the domestic economy of Hindus for corruption and superstition".

7 Kindersley, 231.

8 The Rev. William Ward, 3:86, for example, reacted with the "greatest horror" to the nautch he saw in 1806, condemning the "filthy songs" and dances of "indecent attitudes." And Mrs. Fenton, in 1828, for example, found the nautch quite "odious". *The Journal of Mrs. Fenton,* 241-46, quoted in Nair, *Calcutta in the 19th Century,* 468-69.

9 Quoted in Heber, 1: 47.

10 See Nagendra Nath Ghose, 183-84.

11 Wallace, 264-65, quoted in Nair, *Calcutta in the 19th Century,* 322. Also see Parks, 1:30.

12 From her letter of October 25, 1810, in *Letters on India,* 134-36. Maria Graham was also known as Lady (Maria) Callcott.

13 *Sketches of India*, 211, quoted in Nair, *Calcutta in the 19th Century,* 191.

14 Plate 25, in Losty.

15 Wallace, 265, quoted in Nair, *Calcutta in the 19th Century,* 323.

16 *Sketches of India,* 212-13, quoted in Nair, *Calcutta in the 19th Century,* 192.

17 Quoted in Heber, 1: 47.

18 *Wanderings of a Pilgrim,* 1: 30.

19 *Scenes and Characteristics of Hindostan,* 1: 248-53, quoted in Dyson, 347.

20 *Tribes and Castes of Bengal,* 2: 130.

21 Risley, 2: 129-30.

22 *Tawāyaf + dār,* one who accompanies a courtesan.

23 In the entry under "Bajunia", a class of Muslims, 38-39.

24 "The Voice of the Sarangi", 87-96. Bor includes Solvyns's depiction of the nautch.

2. Rāmjanī

Calcutta: Sec. IV, No. 5. A Ramjanny, or Dancing Girl.
Orme: 11.
Paris: II.3.3. Ramjanny, Dancing Girl.

In the description which I gave in the beginning of the last number, of the original dance which the Hindoos call the *Nautch,* I said that the women who perform it go by the name of *Ramjanny;* but as I did not then take any notice of their costume, I shall here enter into some particulars concerning it.

The dress of the *Ramjannys* is in general very rich and splendid, consisting of precious stuffs embroidered in gold and silver. The under garment is very ample, and generally of coloured silk with lace or embroidery: after turning round several times with great velocity, this sort of petticoat swells out in the form of a sphere, the folds disappear, and the effect is very striking when they let themselves fall and sink as it were into this extended drapery. The richness of their ornaments extends to their toes, which being covered with little bells and moved as they choose, give a pleasing sound and mark the measure of their steps.

I have already observed that formerly the *Ramjannys* were in the service and formed part of the retinue of the Hindoo princes: these young women who were then kept together, under the inspection of a mistress of a more advanced age, were wholly taken up with the study of their profession, and were treated with great respect: but they are now wholly assimilated to the *Bayaderes,* though they still pretend to some preeminence over them: but it is not by their moral conduct that they seek this distinction, for I have often seen them mixed with troops of *Bays* and leading as dissolute a life as any other women of that class. This degeneracy

RĀMJANĪ. Paris II.3.3.

seems to be one of the many effects of the invasion of the Mahometans who spread their luxury and their vices among the conquered people.

COMMENTARY

Solvyns's "Ramjanny" (*rāmjanī*) was not widely used among Europeans as a term for nautch girls and rarely appears in descriptions of the nautch. The origins of the word are disputed. For "Rum-Johnny", obsolete by the late nineteenth century, *Hobson-Jobson,* the glossary of Anglo-Indian words and phrases, gives two meanings. The first applied to the touts who solicited employment from newcomers to Calcutta. The second, "among soldiers and sailors, 'a prostitute'," is derived from Sanskrit, "*rāmā-janī,* 'a pleasing woman,' 'a dancing-girl'."[1] Pran Nevile, who has written on the nautch, gives a formal meaning to *rāmjanī* as those women who know the god Rāmā, but notes that in its usage, mainly in Bihar, it refers to Hindu dancers or courtesans.[2] Sen's *Etymological Dictionary of Bengali,* on the other hand, provides a very different compound origin. For Rām(a)jā̃ni, "a prostitute, courtesan", the origin is from Hindi, *rambhā* (courtesan) plus Perso-Arabian, *zāniya* (whore).[3]

Sherring, in his compendium of Hindu castes, lists "Ramjana, or Rāmjanī", as professional musicians. "They wear the sacred cord, and call themselves Kshatriyas. . . . They also, like the Kathaks, give instruction in singing and dancing to women intending to be professional performers. The caste is devoted to prostitution. The female children born in the caste are brought up to immorality and vice; the sons, however, are trained as musicians, and sometimes engage in trade or other occupations. . . . The Ramjana is a distinct and acknowledged caste, yet it differs from others in admitting women from various casts into the order."[4] Risley provides a brief entry for "Ramjani" in his *Tribes and Castes of Bengal*: "A caste of dancers, singers, and prostitutes" and identifies them as synonymous with the Gandhār, a small caste of musicians, said to be connected with Māls.[5]

Solvyns laments that the distinction between the *rāmjanī* and the "Bayaderes"—dancers he identifies disparagingly with the

Muslim courtesan tradition—had largely disappeared by the late eighteenth century. *Bayadere* is a French word, from the Portuguese *bailadeira,* dancer, but was often used "as if it were a genuine Indian word" by Europeans in India for dancing girls generally.[6] Dr. Francis Buchanan, writing in 1810-11, noted the distinction between Muslim dancing girls called *bai* and the Hindu "rumzani" (*rāmjanī*) in the Bhagalpur district of Bengal.[7] In North India, various names were used for dancers. Muslim dancers, as distinct from the Hindu *rāmjanī,* were often known as *kanchanī,*[8] and the Census distinguished dancers as Paturiya (Hindus) and Tawaif (Muslims).[9]

In his discussion of both the nautch and rāmjanī, Solvyns refers to the princes and "grandees" who formerly maintained troupes of dancing girls. Abu'l-Fazl 'Allāmī, the Mughal emperor Akbar's secretary and historian, describes the "akhārā", "an entertainment held at night by the nobles of this country", and the bands of "natwās" retained in service of the courts.[10]

"Dancing girls", as the Europeans termed them generally, had long been associated with the courtesans of Muslim courts and, however talented as artists, with prostitution, and the musicians associated with them—and the very instruments they played—carried the taint of the profession.[11] Thus, for example, respectable Hindus held the tablā and the sāraṅgī, used in accompaniment to dance, as vulgar or, as Willard described them, "licentious" instruments.[12]

NOTES

1 *Hobson-Jobson,* 773-74. Whitworth, 264, gives the same derivation.

2 Interview, New Delhi, January 1995.

3 804.

4 Sherring, 1:274.

5 Risley, "Ramjani", 2:195, and "Gandhār", 1: 267. Solvyns, I.11.4, portrays the Māls as snake-catchers, but the term is used to include various "gypsy-like" wandering groups.

6 *Hobson-Jobson,* 75. There is no reference to Solvyns's abbreviation, "Bay", but his use suggests its currency in the Calcutta of his time. Shoberl, 3: 53-60, describes the *bayaderes* in dress and dance. His earlier description of the *rāmjanī,* 43-44, paraphrases Solvyns without attribution.

7 Quoted by Bor, "The Voice of the Sarangi", 95-96.
8 Ango-Indian, *cunchunee. Hobson-Jobson,* 280, and under "Dancing Girl", 295-96.
9 Crooke, 4: 364-65.
10 273.
11 Bor, "The Voice of the Sarangi", 81-87.
12 95.

3. Śaṅkh[1] and Ghaṇṭā[2]

Calcutta: Sec. XI, No. 1. A Sunk and G'unta,—used by the Brahmuns at their religious ceremonies.
Orme: 46.
Paris: II.6.2. Sunk and G'unta Musical Instruments.

The instruments which they [the Hindus] use are either for the purposes of religion or of amusement; we will begin by the former. The simplest of the instruments which the Brahmuns use in their temples, is the *sunk,* which is meerly a shell into which they blow with all their strength to call the faithful together. They employ also the *G'unta* for the same purpose: this is a sort of bell of brass, with a head and two wings by way of ornament; they sound it morning and evening, before the sacrifices begin, in the first court of the temple, where there are always some of the images of their divinities, but not always the same: they change them generally every month, and this period is exclusively devoted to their worship, though their festival in reality lasts but eight or ten days, and is celebrated and concluded with the ceremonies which we have already described. After this, each family employs the remainder of the month in devotions to their domestic dieties.

The plate represents a Brahmun standing before the divinity of the month, blowing into the shell, and striking the *G'unta* or bell with his other hand. Other idols are seen, placed on a wooden bench. The figures prostrated on the steps of the altar, in an act of devotion, are also Brahmuns who fulfil this duty before they give themselves up to their private business; for this prayer must of necessity precede all the occupations of the day. That the idea of the Divinity may be ever before their eyes, the Brahmuns are

ŚAṄKH AND GHAṆṬĀ. Paris II.6.2.

commanded never to write on any occasion whatsoever, without having previously written the name of God upon their paper.

The *sunk* or shell is sometimes heard in the bazars or markets; where the Faquirs employ it to announce their arrival.

It is worth remarking that this is the shell of which the *Sunkhaurys* [Śā̃khāri], whose business we have already described in the first volume, make the bracelets of the Hindoo women. The sacred function in which the matter that they employ has been used, gives them a rank in the subdivision of a cast above common artisans.

Commentary

The śaṅkh, or conch shell, obtained from the gastropod Turbinella Pyrum, is used today in precisely the same manner as Solvyns describes. Charles R. Day notes that the conch shell "is said to have been first used by the god Krishna and is mentioned in . . . the Ramayana, where it is called Devadatta. We also find it under the name of Goshringa, both in the Ramayana and Mahabharata".[3]

Frederic Shoberl, in his account of *Hindoostan* in *The World in Miniature*, provides descriptions of musical instruments, drawing principally from Solvyns, with occasional acknowledgment to the artist as his source. On the "sunk", he notes that the shell is "tipped at each end with copper, into which the Brahmins blow for all their might to summon the people to the temples".[4] Copper is deemed to be ritually non-polluting, and the śaṅkh is a notable exception to the general brahminical prohibition against use of wind instruments.

Śā̃khāri (Sankahakara) is the caste of shell-workers, described by Solvyns, I.5.3, who make conch shell bangles. The craft includes decorating the intact conch shell used as a horn. Ashok Mitra, Census Commissioner for West Bengal, states that the craft and the occupational caste is "peculiar to and characteristic of Bengal and Bengali society".[5]

The word *ghaṇṭā* refers to several types of bells, as the sort Solvyns depicts, but it also refers to a plate gong, either hand held or suspended from a support, that is commonly used in temples and sounded in various rituals, especially during *ārtī*, honoring the deity with lighted oil lamps. The gong is used in secular contexts to mark the passing of the hour.

NOTES

1 Dick, "Śaṅkh", NGMI, 3:289-90. Variants: saṅkh, śaṅkha, cankam, caṅku.

2 Dick, "Ghaṇṭā", NGMI, 2:39-40. Variants: ghaṇṭ, ghaṇṭī, ghaṇṭikā, ghaṇṭo.

3 103-4.

4 27.

5 *The Tribes and Castes of West Bengal,* 340-41. Also see Risley, 2: 221-23.

4. Kā̃sar[1]

Calcutta: Sec. XI, No. 2. A Kunser,—beat at stated times by the servants of Priests.
Paris: II.6.3. Kunser. An Other Instrument.

This instrument is used for the same purposes as the two others, and is not less simple: it is nothing more than a piece of brass suspended by a cord; a servant of the temple, even a Brahmun, holds the instrument in one hand, strikes it with a stick sometimes in a quick and sometimes a slow measure, to call together the Hindoos to their sacrifices and other acts of devotion: sounding his *Kunser* till it becomes tiresome. Sometimes the instrument is of a red colour and has a number of small ornaments covered with that beautiful varnish of which the Indians alone possess the secret.

On days of public festivity or *poudjahs* [*pūjās*] the ears are incessantly stunned with the monotonous sound of the *Kunser;* but this instrument is never used at private feasts or rejoicings, nor to celebrate the arrival of a prince or rich Hindoo, as some travellers whose researches have not been very exact upon the countries they traversed, have believed: the Hindoo laws expressly forbid the use of it, except on religious occasions. But the *Kunser* is often confounded with another instrument, the *Kaunsy* [kā̃si, Pl. 29], from the resemblance of the name; a description of which will be given hereafter.

The three instruments which I have just described are consecrated solely to religious purposes: some add also the *khole* [khol, Pl. 15] and the *surmungla* [surmaṇḍal, Pl. 26], but without reason. —We now pass to the description of those which are used for the amusement of private persons, and are infinitely more

KĀSAR. Paris II.6.3.

curious, being more complicated, and some even of a very ingenious invention. As to the *Sunk,* the *G'unta* and the *Kunser,* their noisy sounds scarcely deserve to be honored with the name of music.

COMMENTARY

The more frequently used temple plate gong in Bengal is the ghaṇṭā, which is of consistent thickness, whereas the Bengali kā̃sar is slightly thicker in the center than towards the rim. The instrument takes its name from the material from which it is made, *kā̃sar,* meaning "bell-metal".

Solvyns makes a distinction between kā̃sar, a temple gong, and a similar instrument used on secular occasions that he calls a "kaunsy" (kā̃si, Pl. 29). Today there is little structural or functional difference between the two instruments. This either indicates a loss of specificity in the terms since Solvyns's time or possibly that Solvyns has described usages of the terms restricted to a limited region.

NOTE

1 Dick, "Kā̃sar", NGMI, 2: 362. Variants: kansar, kansi, kā̃si, kā̃sya.

5. Tambūrā[1]

Calcutta: Sec. XI, No. 3. A Tumboora,—played on by the higher orders for their amusements.
Orme: 47.
Paris: II.6.4. Tumboora.

A great deal has been said upon the music of the Hindoos. The Transactions of the Society of Calcutta among others, contain many treatises upon this subject,[2] which is notwithstanding but very imperfectly known in Europe, for this simple reason, that the instruments which they use have never been described with sufficient precision, which ought to have been the principal object, for they are much more remarkable than the music itself. Their instruments have been carried successively to a surprising degree of perfection; but those improvements have not reached their music, which still remains in its infancy. It is impossible not to make this remark in seeing a Hindoo play upon the *Tumboora*; in his hands is a magnificent instrument, covered with paintings and gilding, ornamented to an excess of luxury, and we are naturally led to imagine that he is to draw from it the most enchanting sounds; but on the contrary he remains for hours together in the same attitude, singing a monotonous air, and touching from time to time one of the four chords [strings] which compose this instrument. This is the only use he makes of it, the only pleasure which he seeks from it. And for him even this is a great deal: seated on a carpet or a piece of white cloth, he gives himself up to the pleasing sensations which the vibrations of a single chord produce, and probably he would give up even this enjoyment, if it required the smallest exertion. Everything about him must be proportioned to his natural taste for laziness and indolence.

TAMBŪRĀ, Paris II.6.4.

The *Tumboora* with the rich Hindoos is an object of luxury which they expose frequently in their best rooms, as one of their most precious effects, to attract the eyes of strangers. As to the form of the instrument itself, no description of it is necessary, as I am persuaded that the drawing will give a very sufficient idea of it.

Commentary

Solvyns's misunderstanding of Indian music is nowhere more in evidence than in these comments concerning the tambūrā, the ubiquitous drone instrument of Indian classical music. Looking beyond his disdainful remarks, we find an interesting comment indicating that the tambūrā was looked upon by upper class Hindus as a symbol of wealth. This is most probably related to the patronage of musicians by zamīndārs in Bengal, thus leading to the association of music with the wealthy class and, by extension, the association of the tambūrā with financial well being.

Of the instrument depicted, the presence of a wide bridge of the type used on instruments such as the bīn, sitār, and the modern tambūrā is notable. The system of anchoring the wires and what appears to be a bone decorative guard plate at the base of the sound board, indicating probable use of tuning beads, are similar to those used today and suggest remarkable continuity in construction of the instrument over the past two hundred years.

NOTES

1 Dick, "Tambūrā," NGMI, 3:514-15. Variants: tambūrī, tampūrī, tānpūrā.

2 Solvyns here refers to *Asiatick Researches,* the transactions of the Asiatic Society, that included in the third volume Sir William Jones's article, "On the Musical Modes of the Hindus."

6. Kuplyans or Bīn[1]

Calcutta: Sec. XI, No. 7. A Kuplyaus, or Been,—described in the 1st volume of the Asiatic Researches.
Paris: II.6.5. Kuplyans, or Been.

In order to judge whether the following description is more exact, and consequently more deserving of credit, than that which is inserted in the first volume of the Transactions of the Asiatic Society,[2] it is necessary to inform the reader that I was in possession, while in India, of the instrument in question, and heared it played by the Hindou from whom I purchased it, meaning to bring it over with the rest of my collection, to make it known in Europe: unfortunately it was destroyed by insects so as to frustrate my intentions: but the drawing at least remained such as it is seen in the engraving. The *been* is an instrument composed of two pumpkins of unequal size, dried and cut through the middle, united by a long tube of wood, upon which are stretched several chords of spun cotton gummed, and two of wire; the two pumpkins are joined to the tube which conveys the sound, by other pieces of wood also hollowed out. The instrument is tuned as ours with strings, by turning the pegs fixed in the wood, but the chords are not supported by a bridge, as in the drawing of the Asiatic Society, nor are they so numerous: mine had but four. The musician who played upon it, a Brahmun, of *Mursadabad* in Bengal, had very strong nails and of a great length: with one hand he pinched with his nails the chords below, and with the other he pressed them above, striking them also at times with a little stick. I can affirm that the sounds produced by this singular instrument, are very sweet and harmonious, especially in the higher notes. I am even persuaded that this musician would have

KUPLYANS or BĪN. Paris II.6.5.

been heard with pleasure in an European concert: it is true that he had in the country the reputation of excelling on this instrument, and was consequently capable of giving me all the information which I might require.

None of the *beens* which I had an opportunity of seeing during my residence in Asia, resembled that given by the Asiatic Society, and I was always careful to compare them. The instrument is nevertheless of true Hindoo origin, and is properly played only in the countries inhabited by primitive Hindoos, I cannot therefore conceive why in the drawing of the Society it is in the hands of a Mussulman.

Commentary

Hindu mythology relates that the sage Narada, son of Brahmā and leader of the celestial musicians, invented the vīṇā,[3] and Sarasvatī, goddess of learning and patroness of music, plays the vīṇā, one of her iconographical attributes as she is represented in painting, sculpture, and sacred images.

The vīṇā is the first Indian musical instrument to receive detailed discussion by European travellers and scholars. Pietro Della Valle (1586-1652) describes the instrument in the account of his travels to India, and Marin Mersenne includes the vīṇā in his seventeenth century treatise on music, *Harmonie Universelle.*[4] The most extensive early European description (referred to above by Solvyns) is Francis Fowke's "On the Vina, or Indian Lyre", published in the first volume of *Asiatick Researches* in 1788, with an engraving depicting the instrument itself and another as it is played.[5] In that same volume, Sir William Jones, in writing "On the Gods of *Greece, Italy,* and *India*", includes an engraving of Narada playing the vīṇā and quotes from the poem *Magha:*[6] "*Nāred* [Narada] sat watching from time to time his large *Vīnā,* which by impulse of the breeze, yielded notes that pierced successively the regions of his ear, and proceeded by musical intervals".[7]

Solvyns refers to Narada's invention of the vīṇā in his Introduction to *Les Hindoûs,* Vol. II,[8] but makes no mention of the instrument's association with Sarasvatī. His concern in the descriptive text accompanying the plate here is with the instrument itself. Another early European artist, Charles Gold, working in South India at the time Solvyns was in Bengal, also portrayed the instrument in a drawing, published later as a print.[9]

The name *kuplyans*, used by Solvyns, is limited to Bengal and, as far as we are aware, appears nowhere else in reference to a stick zither type instrument. It is notable that Solvyns was unaware of the fretted variety of stick zither, also known as bīn, that was popular in the Mughal courts. It is possible that the fretted bīn had entered its period of decline by the time of Solvyns's visit to India, but the instrument seems to have been available to later writers. Perhaps it was less known in Bengal than in the heartland.

Concerning Solvyns's description of the instrument, in which he gives the number of strings as four (two of wire, two of gummed cotton), the print indicates that two strings were approximately half the length of the others. It is probable that these served a drone function in the same manner as the *cikārī* strings of the modern vīṇā and sitār. It is also to be noted that the instrument pictured lacks any bridge. The strings are simply anchored to small posts projecting from the carved end of the stick body. This part is carved in the shape of a swan head, possibly indicating some connection with the goddess Sarasvatī, whose vehicle is the swan. However, what is most interesting about Solvyns's bīn is that the instrument is played both with a wooden slide and by pressing with the fingers of the left hand. These methods of pitch production existed on the ekatantrī vīṇā (a one-stringed stick zither with a gourd resonator) described in the *Saṅgitaratnākara* by the thirteenth century musicologist Śārṅgadeva.[10] A stick zither called sar-vīṇā, possibly played in a similar manner, is mentioned in the *Ā'īn-i-Akbarī* of Abu'l-Fazl 'Allāmī, court chronicler of Akbar.[11] Mention of this playing technique in the late eighteenth century gives us evidence that the modern vicitrā vīṇā, or baṭṭu vīṇā, which is thought to have been "invented" in the nineteenth century, is a direct lineal descendent of an earlier indigenous instrument. In essence, the Solvyns bīn provides us with a missing link that suggests the continous existence of a fretless stick zither played with a slide on the Indian subcontinent since the thirteenth century.

NOTES

1 The instrument is described in NGMI under the name by which it is most widely known, vīṇā: Dick, Geekie, and Widdess, "Vīṇā", 3: 728-35.
2 Fowke, "On the *Vina*, or *Indian* Lyre" (1788). Perhaps the earliest European description is by Pietro Della Valle (1586-1652) in his *Travels*, 1: 117-18.
3 Daniélou, 187.
4 For a discussion of these early descriptions of the vīṇā, see Bor, "The Rise of Ethnomusicology", 52-53.
5 Fowke. The plate appears opposite, p. 252.
6 Jones refers to the *Sisupalavadha* (*Maghakavya*) by the seventh century poet Magha.
7 1: 227.
8 See Solvyns's reference to Narada in our Introduction, p. 5.
9 *Oriental Drawings*, Plate 22, "A Satadevan, accompanied by his son dancing". The figure is portrayed playing a vīṇā.
10 3: 233-38.
11 Abu'l-Fazl 'Allāmī, 269.

7. Pināk[1]

Calcutta: Sec. XI, No. 8. Pennauck,—the shell of a large Pumkin, and half the shell of a small one joined together by an iron wire.
Orme: 50.[2]
Paris: II.6.6. Pennauck

This is also a very singular instrument, and very different from those which we use in Europe. The form of the *Pennauck* is not unlike that of the *been* of which we have just been speaking, being likewise composed of two pumpkins; but they are joined by an iron rod, and one of them is much larger, and forms consequently a wider aperture than the other: the smaller is at the bottom, the larger at top. The essential difference between this instrument and the *been* is that, in the place of chords it has but one string of wire, strongly stretched. To draw out the sound, a bow like that of a base is prest upon this chord, at the same time that another part of it is struck or rubbed with a little stick. I confess that this strange music is far from being agreeable, and can be pleasing only to the ear of an Hindoo.

The *Pennauck* is now as seldom heard in India as in the other provinces of Asia; it is not even easy to find a musician who knows how to play upon it. The same may be said of the *been*. In former times both these instruments were much in vogue, and I have been assured that those who excelled in playing them were held in a certain degree of consideration, which has lasted even to our times. The masters of the *been* and the *Pennauck* being very few, are treated with great respect, and people flock round them to hear their singular music as a curiosity. They are to be heard only with the rich, as they never play for money before the public. I take it for granted that it is not necessary to repeat here, that

PINAK. Paris II.6.6.

I profess to treat only of true Hindoos: it is no concern of mine if the Mussulmen have, or have not appropriated to themselves these instruments, and use them as means of earning their bread. My purpose is to make known only what relates to the Hindoo people exclusively: I must therefore be careful to distinguish their customs from those of their oppressors.

Commentary

The word *pinākī* means "bow" and is associated with the god Śiva. As Solvyns portrays the instrument, it is essentially a bowed bīn. The pināk, most widely known as the pinākī vīṇā, is described in detail in the *Saṅgitaratnākara* [3] and is mentioned as the pināk in the *Ā'īn-i-Akbarī*.[4] Solvyns informs us that this instrument and the preceding bīn were objects of great prestige and status among Hindus, that the musicians who specialized on these instruments were non-professionals, and that the instruments themselves were nearing extinction in Hindu culture at the time of his writing. The pinākī vīṇā appears to have disappeared completely from Hindustani music culture in the early nineteenth century. It is not mentioned by Willard,[5] nor is it mentioned by later nineteenth century writers. Indeed, as Joep Bor writes, Solvyns provides us with what is probably the last description of the instrument.[6]

NOTES

1 Dick, "Pināk", NGMI, 3: 113; also see under "Vīṇā", NGMI, 3: 731. Variants: pināka, pinākī.

2 The Orme plate's title, "Pennauck, or Been", recognizes no distinction between the two instruments, and the confusion is evidenced by the plate's slightly modified copy of Solvyns's one-stringed, fretless pināk, while the text describes a seven-stringed bīn. In contrast to Solvyns's portrayal and description of the pināk's lower gourd as smaller, the two gourds depicted in the Orme plate are of roughly equal size, and the accompanying text gives their dimensions as the same. The Orme text, without attribution, is drawn from Francis Fowke's description of the bīn in the first volume of *Asiatick Researches* (1788).

3 3: 314-17.

4 Abu'l-Fazl 'Allāmī, 269.

5 "A Treatise on the Music of Hindoostan" (1834).

6 "The Voice of the Sarangi", 41. Among the numerous illustrations in this volume, Bor includes Solvyns's depictions of five bowed instruments, including the pinā̄k, and writes, "Despite his [Solvyns's] lack of understanding of the music . . . his descriptions reveal information which is to be found nowhere else, and particularly so in those cases where the instruments have become obsolete," 71.

8. Sitār[1]

Calcutta: Sec. XI, No. 4. A Sittar, or Guittar.
Orme: 48.
Paris: II.7.2. A Sittar, or Guittar.

To resume the subject of the preceding number, the instrument called *Sittar* or *Guittar,* resembles very much our guitar as well in its form as in its name. I am even uncertain whether it is originally Hindoo: I have been assured of the contrary, but the assertion remains without proof. An European would make much more of this instrument than the Hindoo musicians, who are satisfied with touching the chords meerly from time to time; and as they are much more charmed with the noise than with the melody of their music, they frequently, to create a variety in their dull and monotonous sounds, place an iron ring in each chord of the *Sittar,* which being put in motion by the vibration, and striking against each other, produces a singular noise which delights the ear of the Hindoos, and appears to them the supreme degree of perfection.

The *Sittar* is now seldom used in India; perhaps the better sort of Hindoos have taken it in aversion since the *Loutchias,* or people of dissolute manners, have taken to playing it for money, and have chosen this music to accompany their obscene songs and other immoral practices. At their feasts, the *Nautch,* a dance which we have described in the second number of this volume, is sometimes performed to the sound of the *Sittar,* and some tolerable musicians, or rather meer players upon it, may be heard.

The Mussulmen have taken up this instrument as they have the others, and if a traveller by chance hears the *Sittar,* he may be pretty certain that it is played by one of them.

SITĀR. Paris II.7.2.

COMMENTARY

Alastair Dick traces the history of the Indian sitār to the tanbūr of the early Muslim sultanates in India, postulating that the Indian sitār and the Uzbek dutar share a common ancestor. He bases his argument on structural similarities exhibited by the two instruments. The tanbūr eventually was known as tanbūrah. From various references in court chronicles, we know that the tanbūrah was a popular instrument in the Mughal courts and was adopted by Hindu musicians of the highest rank (Kalavant) by the seventeenth century.[2] How or why this instrument came to be known as the sitār, if indeed that was the case, remains obscured. Dick suggests that there might have been a three-stringed tanbūr known as sihtār-tanbūr (*sihtār* indicating three strings) whose name was eventually shortened to sihtār and then sitār. We do not hear of specialists on the sitār until the mid-eighteenth century, when Masit Khan established the style of playing on the instrument known today as the *masīkhānī bāj*. According to some authorities, it was Masit Khan who added two strings to an earlier three-stringed instrument to invent the sitār. Another popular story attributes the invention of the instrument to Amir Khusrau Khan, a musician in the Delhi court of Muhammad Shah, the Mughal emperor, who ruled from 1719 to 1748. Willard's reference in 1834 to the sitār as a modern instrument (but invented by Umeer Khosro [Amir Khusro] of Delhi) gives somewhat contradictory evidence that at least the use of the term *sitār* to designate this instrument was still relatively new.[3]

Solvyns's comments about the sitār indicate that the instrument was used in at least two different social and musical contexts: as an accompanying instrument in courtesan dancing and as a solo instrument of professional Muslim musicians, presumably of the courts. It appears also to have been an instrument known to unskilled amateur musicians in urban society who dawdled upon it, trying new ways (such as placing iron rings on the strings) to produce amusing sounds.

It is known that the number of strings on the sitār was increased during the course of its evolution. The instrument pictured here had six strings. Twelve frets can be discerned in close examination of the etching, but it is not possible to determine if these were of the raised, arched type used today or were simply tied gut frets as found on Middle Eastern lutes. The joint connecting the gourd (*tumbā*) to the wooden "shoulder", which in turn connects to the neck, is clearly visible in the etching. The noticeable absence of the wide bridge used on modern instruments supports the assertion that the Indian sitār was developed from an imported instrument by overlaying features of the bīn. On the other hand, the presence of a double-nut and added tuning beads (could Solvyns have mistaken these as the source of jangling?), along with the considerable size of the instrument and the relatively wide neck, clearly indicates that many features of the modern sitār are at least two hundred years old.

If the sitār developed from the tanbūr of the Mughal courts, it remains unexplained how the instrument entered the society of the "loutchias" (Bengali, *loccā*; Hindi, *luccā*, meaning a vile, wanton person)[4] mentioned by Solvyns and subsequently acquired much of the social stigma among Hindus of the time that attached to other instruments used by these people. One possibility might be that many of these people were illegitimate offspring of the court dancing girls who, forced to leave the court because of economic decline, gravitated to the brothel districts of urban centers and took with them remnants of the court life they had experienced in their youth.

It is not clear if Solvyns uses *loutchia* as a term for a specific group or simply as a descriptive noun applicable to any dissolute individual no matter what his origins may be. *Hobson-Jobson* states that the term *loocher* is often used in Anglo-Indian colloquial as "a blackguard libertine, a lewd loafter". No caste or community identity is inferred.[5] Be that as it may, Solvyns's "loutchias" appear to have been a musician group in close association with the courtesans. They were drawn from both Hindu and Muslim sectors of the society and, in addition to the sitār, played the tablā[6] and the sāraṅgī.[7]

Solvyns notes that the Hindu musicians had adopted some of the sartorial tastes of the Muslims, possibly a vestige of life during Muslim court patronage. The sitār's low status among the *bīnkār* (musicians specializing on the bīn) of the Mughal courts can be explained if we assume that the instrument entered court life in the hands of low class accompanists of dancers, or possibly as an instrument that accompanied the songs of vocalists of lesser rank than the Kalavant singers of *dhrupad*, the most important genre of North Indian classical music of that period. As the *bīnkār* improved upon the instrument by adding to it various features of the bīn, the sitār became more popular and more versatile as a solo instrument. A tremendous transformation in the instrument's popularity ensued during the nineteenth century. Willard, who was "in the service" of the Nawab of Banda, a court in what is now Madhya Pradesh renowned for the famous *bīnkār* and *sitāriyā* musicians who were in its employ during the nineteenth century, indicates that the instrument was admired by professionals and amateurs alike.[8] Charles. R. Day, writing nearly a century after Solvyns, states that the "sitār is called also Sundari, and is perhaps the commonest of all the stringed instruments in India, being much admired".[9] Apparently, the instrument had acquired such high cultural esteem through its association with the *bīnkār* musicians that its intermediate history as an instrument of the "louchias" was soon forgotten.

NOTES

1 Dick, "Sitar", NGMI, 3: 392-400. Urdu, Hindi, Gujarati, sitār; Bengali, setār; Marathi, satār. On the history of the instrument, see Miner, *Sitar and Sarod in the 18th and 19th Centuries*, and "The Sitār: An Overview of Change", 27-57. In both the book and article, Miner refers to Solvyns and reproduces the etching.

2 Dick, "Sitar", 292-93.

3 Willard, 98.

4 Sen, 826, derives the word from the Persian *lucha*. The English *lout*, an ill-mannered fellow, is obviously similar, but *The Oxford English Dictionary* makes no etymological connection.

5 519.

6 Plate 17.

7 Plate 9.

8 98.

9 Day, 117.

9. Sāraṅgī[1]

Calcutta: Sec. XI, No. 16. Saringee,—played at Nautches, &c.
Orme: 51.
Paris: II.7.3. Saringee.

This instrument, which is frequently met with in every part of Hindoostan, is very like the violoncello, though it is smaller and has more chords. The sounds which it produces are soft and melodious, and susceptible of greater variety than those of the other instruments. Of all the different kinds of Hindoo music in general, the *Saringee* comes nearest to that of Europe. The chords are of spun cotton; the pieces of wood which form the instrument are united by a very fine white skin glued over the joints. The sweet sounds of the *Saringee* are well adapted to accompany the voice; it is used in all the dances both of men and women.

The *louchias* too are the most frequent performers on this instrument; for which reason in the back-ground of the print I have represented a house of bad fame, and a woman of the vilest class, because such is the general resort of the *louchias,* where they give themselves up to every excess of debauchery. They are sunk to such a degree of degradation, that they respect neither their national manners nor dress. Some of them, though of Hindoo origin, dress like Mussulmen, or rather like the Mogols of the north of India, others, though by birth they are Mussulmen, pass their lives with the most corrupt of the Hindoos.

These *louchias* are much more despised in Hindoostan, than the female prostitutes with whom they constantly consort. In general, the irregularities of women meet with less contempt here than in Europe; the heat of the climate is supposed to operate as an incitement to vice, and by encreasing the number

SĀRAṄGĪ. Paris II.7.3.

of its votaries, seems to exempt it from that degree of horror which it inspires when it is confined to a few miserable wretches. Many Hindoo women are destined from their infancy to this abominable trade, and carry it on without having an idea of its immorality.

COMMENTARY

In his descriptive note on the sāraṅgī in the 1799 *Catalogue*, Solvyns writes simply that it is played at nautchs, and in his print portraying the dance (Pl. 1), Solvyns includes a sāraṅgī among the instruments.

The sāraṅgī is believed to have originated as a folk instrument. This view is supported by the widespread use of it, in a variety of forms, in folk cultures of different regions of South Asia. Its suitability as a melodic accompanying instrument for voice promoted its popularity among singers of the classical *khayāl* in the princely courts. That popularity greatly diminished, however, partly because of the instrument's association with courtesan life. This association seems to have been well-established by the end of the eighteenth century, as is evidenced by Solvyns's assertion that the "*loutchias* are the most frequent performers on the instrument". Day, a century later, writes that the sāraṅgī "is considered to be rather vulgar, and hence musicians, though they admire and like it very much, will usually employ either a low caste Hindu or a Mussulman to play it".[2]

Solvyns makes frequent reference to the low status of most musicians, both Hindu and Muslim, and to the disrepute in which they are held. "Musicians are regarded all over India as a debased race," ethnographer James Wise wrote in 1883, "and in Eastern Bengal Muhammadan musicians are either barbers (jajjām), or the husbands of midwives (dāi), classes ranked among the vilest of the population."[3]

NOTES

1 Sorrell and Helffer, "Sāraṅgī", NGMI, 3: 294-96. Variants: sāraṅg, hārangī. For a rich portrayal of the instrument and its traditions, see Bor, "The Voice of the Sarangi". Bor draws extensively on

Indian painting and includes, in addition to various European depictions of the sāraṅgī as a part of nautch performances, Solvyns's sāraṅgī etching. He provides, as well, references to the instrument by European travellers as early as the seventeenth century.

2 125.

3 In the entry under "Bājunia", a class of Muslims, 38.

10. Sārindā[1]

Calcutta: Sec. XI, No. 5. A Sarinda or Violin,—the most common Hindostanee musical instrument.
Orme: 49.
Paris: II.7.4. Sarinda.

As the *Tumboora* and the *Been* are the instruments of the richer class of Hindoos, so that which we are going to speak of under the name of *Sarinda* belongs almost exclusively to the poor: in so much, that most of the common people, particularly the palanquin bearers, have one of them of their own making: this does not require much genius, being no more than a bit of wood hollowed out, over which are stretched some chords of spun cotton: and the sound is produced by drawing over them a bow, as represented in the print. The music is proportioned to the rudeness of the instrument, and can be pleasing only to its Hindoo inventers. Few of those who play upon the *Sarinda* have any knowledge of music; they meerly follow their fancy, continuing sometimes in a lower tone with deep expression, at others rising suddenly from the lowest to the highest notes in reiterated cadences, but always without taste, measure or harmony.

I have just observed that the *Sarinda* is the ordinary amusement of the palanquin bearers: the person I have represented is one of them: he stands on a little platform before the door of his employer; this the place generally allowed to these servants; the houka [*hũkā*] alone which he has by him is a sufficient indication of his condition.[2]

If his amusements are ill suited to our European taste, we must however acknowledge that they cannot be more innocent, and

SĀRINDĀ. Paris II.7.4.

that the diversions of persons of the same rank among us are neither so harmless nor so easily attained.

COMMENTARY

The sāriṅdā continues to exist in the same form today as pictured in Solvyns's etching. An instrument of identical shape is pictured by Day, who writes that it "is common in Bengal. . . . The Sarinda is not a very high-class instrument, but is very popular with the lower classes."[3] In *The Costume of Indoostan*, Orme's pirated edition of the Solvyns etchings, the text for the plate describes the sāriṅdā as "the most common musical instrument in Hindostan. Its effect is neither unpleasant, nor captivating; and it is in general performed on by those who have little ear, or less taste, and may class with the blind fidlers at country wakes."[4]

Palanquin bearers in Bengal, associated with the instrument, were drawn from various castes, typically lower, often "untouchable", castes, and especially from the various Jāliyā (Jellee in Solvyns, I.7.5) fishermen castes. The Duliā (Doolee in Solvyns, I.7.4), a subcaste of the Bāgdi fishermen caste, are traditionally palanquin bearers, but neither Solvyns nor Risley, in his *Tribes and Castes of Bengal*,[5] refer to music in association with these groups.

NOTES

1 Baily and Dick, "Sārindā", NGMI, 3: 297-98. Also see Bor, "The Voice of the Sarangi", 13-17, and with reference to Solvyns, 71.

2 The *hūkā* (Anglo-Indian, hooka or hubble-bubble), to the left behind the figure in the etching, is a pipe in which the smoke is cooled as it is drawn through water. See *Hobson-Jobson*, 423-24. The *hūkā* shown here, with its coiled "snake" or tube, is of the better sort and would be indicative of lower social status only by its unadorned simplicity. Solvyns depicts various forms of the *hūkā* in Vol. III of *Les Hindoûs*.

3 125.

4 Plate 49.

5 I: 37-41.

11. Amṛti [Omerti][1]

Calcutta: Sec. XI, No. 9. Omerti,—kind of Fiddle.
Paris: II.7.5. OMORTI.

This is also an instrument with strings; but what renders it more curious, and proves it of Hindoo origin is, that the body of the instrument is made of a cocoa-nut, cut down to about one-third, and covered over with a very fine skin. To this species of tymbal, is joined a wooden handle with strings stretched from one end of the instrument to the other; there is the whole secret of this truely Hindoo invention. The man who plays it, is seated, holds it between his knees, and endeavours to draw musical sounds from the shell of his cocoa-nut. At a distance it would be difficult to form a guess at what he is about, and still harder to conceive that it is an amusement. The sound of the *Omerti* is not unlike that of the *Sarinda* and the *Saringee,* but something sweeter and less grating to the ear of an European. One is not a little surprised to hear a tolerably harmonious music from a cocoa-shell.

The praises which I heard a skilful Brahmun bestow on a concert of *Omertis* of different sizes, made me curious to assemble one in order to judge of the truth of his assertions; the more so, as the Brahmun himself was really an excellent performer, and I imagined that a reunion of several such as he, might have rather a fine effect: but this instrument being very rare, I could with difficulty find but three, and those very indifferent and far inferior to him; so that my hope was deceived.

This instrument is unknown to many Hindoos, though some among the higher classes, play on it for their amusement.

AMṚTI. Paris II.7.5.

COMMENTARY

The amṛti—"omerti" to Solvyns's ear—was already in decline in the late eighteenth century, and Joep Bor suggests that it "must have vanished" soon after Solvyns portrayed it.[2] References to the amṛti are few, but the *Ā'īn-i-Akbarī* briefly describes the instrument as having one gourd and a single iron string[3]—clearly different from the amṛti Solvyns portrays. Solvyns's reference to its use by "higher classes . . . for their amusement" indicates that the amṛti might be a predecessor of the esrāj, a hybrid instrument combining the fretted neck of the sitār with the waisted, skin-covered resonator of the Bengali dotār and the bow of the Western cello.[4] As pictured, the amṛti appears to have had at least four strings, indicating a potential pitch range of two or more octaves. The bow appears to be similar to that used for the sāraṅgī and other indigenous bowed instruments.

Amṛti is used today as a term for the rāvaṇhatthā, a spike fiddle,[5] and Bor notes a similarity in the instrument Solvyns portrays to the "ravanastron" (rāvaṇhatthā) depicted by Pierre Sonnerat in 1782.[6]

Deben Bhattacharya writes that Solvyns's description and illustration suggest similarity to the keñkariyā from Bundelkhand in central India. "The term 'Kenkār' means the cry of the swan and also the noise of scraping metal with other objects. The fiddle 'Keñkariyā' has a belly of split coconut covered with skin and a long wooden neck bearing one melody string made of a strand of horsetail hair and seven sympathetic strings of metal. It is played with a hunter's bow (as in the picture) which is also made of horsetail hair."[7]

NOTES

1 NGMI, 1: 56. Variation: amriti. Solvyns's titles it "Omorti" in the Paris edition, but in the text (as in the Calcutta edition) spells it "Omerti".

2 "The Voice of the Sarangi", 73. Bor notes that the last reference he found to the amṛti was by S. N. Tagore in 1877, and "it is doubtful if he ever saw any such instrument".

3 See Dick, "Sirbīṇ", NGMI, 3: 390, and Bor, "The Voice of the Sarangi", 75.

4 Dick, "Esrāj", NGMI, 1: 719.

5 See Dick and Sorrell, "Rāvaṇhatthā", NGMI, 3: 198-99. Variant: rāvaṇhasta.

6 Bor, "The Voice of the Sarangi", 75. The instrument is illustrated in plate 40, in Bor, 46. See Sonnerat, *Voyage aux Indes Orientales et a la Chine*, 1: 178-81. A plate in the original, French edition depicts various musical instruments, but the plates are not included with the English translation.

7 Letter to author, 17 February, 1992.

12. Oorni

Calcutta: Sec. XI, No. 35. An Oorni, from the Coromandel Coast.
Orme: 28.[1]
Paris: II.7.6. Oorni.

The *Oorni* scarcely deserves the name of a musical instrument, and I should not have noticed it, but that it is commom all through India, especially on the coast of Coromandel: but in the great towns, such as Calcutta, Madras, Bombay, it is seldom seen but in the hands of *Says* (stable-boys) *Haurrys,* (nightmen), and others of the lowest ranks. The print suffices to shew that the *Oorni* is nothing more than an open cocoa-nut to which a hollow stick of bambou is applied, and one chord which they scrape with a bow often loaded with ornaments. The sound of this music, if it may be called by that name, cannot be compared to any thing better than to the crying of a cat or of a wild beast; the same note is heard for several minutes, and is followed by another higher or lower, but always as shrill and as monotonous. This does not prevent the lower classes of Hindoos from entertaining a high opinion of their *Oorni,* and even imagining that nothing can be more charming to the ear of Europeans. With this idea they frequently come and play it under the windows of their houses, and to render the concert more complete, mingle with it the no less harsh and discordant sound of their own voices. I have been sometimes so stunned with it, that I have been obliged to send out my servants to drive off these execrable musicians.

OORNI. Paris II.7.6.

Commentary

While the amṛti was an instrument associated with the higher classes, the oorni seems to have been restricted to the lower castes. Such one-stringed bowed lutes can be found throughout North Indian folk cultures under various names, but the term *oorni* may be either specious or obsolete. In the area of Bengal, the bena of the Rajbansi people closely resembles Solvyns's description of the oorni.[2] The bow depicted in the Solvyns portrait appears to have a set of bells (ghuṅgrū) attached to it. Such bows are still common in folk cultures of North India.

The oorni also appears similar to the ektāra,[3] a one-stringed instrument made from a gourd or of wood, with one side open. It is widely used in Bengal, notably among the Bauls, wandering minstrels, in accompanying their devotional songs.[4]

Shoberl writes that "The oorni yields but two sounds, one of which is described as resembling the mewing of a cat, and the other the lowing of deer."[5]

Solvyns's "Says" [Bengali, *sahis*] is syce, or groom.[6] "Hurry" is Hāṛi, which Risley describes as "a menial and scavenger caste of Bengal" and whose various occupations include "playing of instruments at weddings and festivals".[7]

NOTES

1 The Orme text accompanying the plate depicting the oorni mistakingly identifies it as the "Bansee" and follows the description from the Solvyns 1799 *Catalogue* for the bamboo flute (Calcutta: Sec. XI, No. 36).

2 Sanyal.

3 Dick, Babiracki, and Helffer, "Ektār", NGMI, 1: 649-50.

4 On the Bauls, see Capwell.

5 3: 30.

6 Solvyns, IV.4.2.

7 1: 316. Solvyns portrays the Hāṛi, I.12.4

13. Ḍhāk[1]

Calcutta: Sec. XI, No. 21. D'Hauk,—used at Marriages and Religious ceremonies.
Orme: 55.
Paris: II.8.2. D'Hauck.

I have yet many musical instruments to describe: this engraving represents the *D'Hauck,* an enormous drum which a single man finds it difficult to carry. The Hindoo who plays upon it has two sticks with which he strikes the skin of the drum quicker or slower, as he fancies, and sometimes with astonishing velocity. It must be observed that the *D'Hauck* is a privileged instrument; that is to say, that it cannot be played without an autorisation from the *Jummadar* [*jamādār*] of the place: this permission is not obtained without a certain retribution, and only on great festivals, marriages, etc. The *D'Hauck* is particularly suited to the Hindoo people, who are extremely fond of noisy instruments; they are delighted with its hollow sounds, and think that nothing can surpass them.

On days of great ceremony, such as the *Durgah* [*Durgā*], *Calkee* [*Kālī*], *J'haump,* [*Jhāmp*], *Churrack* [*Caṛak*], they ornament the *D'Hauck* with plumes and horsehair, which encreases its preposterous size.

It is with this instrument that they who give the feast of the *Churrack* assemble the persons who choose to perform the swinging which we have described in the twelfth number of the first volume. Some days before the ceremony, they are led in procession through their quarter, to the sound of the *D'Hauck.* It sometimes happens that the courage of these devotees not being equal to their piety, they begin by following the drum slowly and trembling; but soon its noisy sounds and the fumes of intoxicating

ḌHĀK. Paris II.8.2.

liquors, animate them, and exalt their imagination to a degree of intrepidity which allows them to see only the glory which is to attend this fanatical undertaking.

COMMENTARY

The term *ḍhāk* has been used since medieval times in reference to various types of Indian drums. The Bengali ḍhāk, depicted by Solvyns, is a large drum, often decorated with feathers, that continues to be played in association with Śaiva-Śākta religious festivals.[2] Solvyns refers to their use in such festivals as Durgā Pūjā and Kālī Pūjā. (His "Calkee" is clearly meant to be Kālī, as Kalki, the last and yet-to-come avatar of Viṣṇu, is not celebrated in festival.) In a separate etching (I.10.1), not included here, Solvyns depicts Jhāmp, part of the Gājan festival dedicated to Śiva, and prominently portrays several ḍhāks. At Jhāmp, Hindus in expiation of their sins throw themselves from scaffolds onto mattresses (*jhāmp*) in which sharp instruments are inserted. Caṛak Pūjā is the hook-swinging festival, also part of Gājan, that attracted large crowds and drew the particular interest of Europeans before the British suppressed the practice in the nineteenth century. Solvyns, in the text accompanying the Caṛak Pūjā plate (I.12.1), describes it as consisting "in getting the flesh bored under the bladebone by two iron hooks fastened by a rope to a lever poised on the top of a sort of mast. By applying a weight to the other branch of the lever, the patient is elevated to the height of about thirty feet, and whirled round as many times as his zeal prompts him, or his strength permits him to bear."

Today ḍhāks are seen most prominently in Bengal at Durgā Pūjā and are typically accompanied by a kā̃sar (Pl. 4) [kā̃sī (Pl. 29)], or gong. The *ḍhākis,* as the players are known, are usually from the low Bauri and Bayen castes, and they often dance to the rhythmic beat of their drums.[3] Traditionally, though no longer today, the master *ḍhāki* would be "sumptuously remunerated" during Durgā Pūjā.[4]

The term *jamādār,* from the Persian, refers to the head of any body of men and in Bengal, in Solvyns's time, had various meanings depending on context. Here Solvyns probably refers to the *zamīndār*, or landholder. In Bengal in the late eighteenth century, the two words seem to have been conflated. *Hobson-Jobson* notes that at that time the prevailing pronunciation of *zamīndār* was indistinguishable from *jamādār*.[5]

NOTES

1 Dick, Babiracki, and Dournon, "Ḍhāk", NGMI, 1:559. Variants: ḍhā̃k, ḍhākkā, ḍeru.
2 Ray, *Folk-Music of Eastern India*, 41.
3 Prabhas Sen, 128. A large color photograph, 128-29, depicts the *ḍhākis* with their plumed drums.
4 Ray, *Music of Eastern India*, 105.
5 980.

14. Ḍhol[1]

Calcutta: Sec. XI, No. 25. A D'Hola,—beaten on one side by the hand, and on the other by a stick.
Paris: II.8.3. D'Hola.

This also is a sort of drum, but smaller than the *D'Hauck* [*ḍhāk*]. It is beaten on the upper skin with the hand, and on the lower with a stick; the sound is dead, and serves only for accompanying: it is used at all their feasts and with every sort of music; so that it is universally known among the Hindoos.

It may easily be supposed that it does not require much art to play upon it; for which reason many of the lower classes abandon their trades, by which they earned a moderate but competent subsistance, to become *D'Hola* players; a profession which suits their indolent disposition, promises them an easy life and all the pleasures that accord with the grossness of their taste. The liquors and portions of *pawn* [*pān*] which those who give feasts are in the habit of distributing to them must necessarily ruin the health of these unhappy people by continual and immoderate use. Their wives and children too, by partaking of the profusion of these donations, contract habits of debauchery. As these feasts always take place in the night, they can sleep but in the day. This continual fatigue and sitting up, and still more the excessive use of strong liquors by which they think to recruit their strength, gives them a pale and livid complexion, and renders them for ever indisposed and unfit for labour. The greater part of these unfortunate beings sink into a state of absolute stupidity, and are soon branded by their countrymen with the contemptuous appellation of *Pariahs*.

The form of the *D'Hola* is the same all through Hindoostan,

ḌHOL. Paris II.8.3.

and differs only in its ornaments: they generally cover this instrument, as they do all the others, with a red cloath, to preserve it from the damp and the dust.

COMMENTARY

Although correctly identified in the Calcutta edition, Solvyns mislabels and reverses the plates for the ḍhol and the ḍholak in the Paris edition. The ḍhol, depicted here, is usually larger than the ḍholak and has a ratio of length to head diameter in the range of 5:4. The drummer hangs the drum from his neck, and it is commonly played, as Solvyns notes, with a combination hand and stick technique, with the left hand striking the higher pitched head (usually above or to the right) and, in the right hand, the stick striking or scraping the lower pitched head (below or to the left). The stick is traditionally of bamboo, with a curved or hooked head.[2]

Contrary to what Solvyns asserts, the ḍhol is not the same throughout India. Alastair Dick establishes two lineages of ḍhol in South Asia: a shallow barrel type stemming from West Asian influence with a head to body length ratio of 1:1 or less, and larger barrel drums stemming from the paṭaha, a drum of ancient and medieval India. Examples of the first type include the Rajasthani ḍhol and the ḍhol of Garhwal, Uttar Pradesh.[3] The Bengali ḍhol is an example of the second type.

The "pawn" chewed by Solvyns's "informants" is *pān*, a mildly narcotic preparation of betel, acrea nut, lime, etc., wrapped in a betel leaf and chewed.[4]

Drummers and musicians more generally were often from "untouchable" castes, such as, in Bengal, Mucī (I.12.3), Hāṛi (I.12.4), and Dom (I.11.6). The term *pariah* derives from the untouchable Paraiyar caste of south India. The Tamil *parai* means drum, and members of the caste traditionally drummed at festivals, but Solvyns's use of *pariah* conveys no such association. He states in his discussion of the śudrā (I.2.6) that "the term *Parriah* is a demonation which denotes in general everthing which is worst.... There are *Parriahs* therefore in every cast, but there is no particular cast of *Parriahs*." Though not present in

Bengal, there is surely a Paraiyar caste in the south, but *Hobson-Jobson* indicates that "the name *pariah* has come to be regarded as applicable to the whole body of the lowest castes. . . . The mistaken use of pariah, as synonymous with out-caste has spread in English parlance all over India", and this usage goes back as far as the sixteenth century.[5]

Drumming in the late eighteenth century, however, was not confined to the low castes. In his discussion of "A Woman of Distinction" (II.2.2), Solvyns writes that "sometimes . . . , at intervals only, she will relieve the monotomy of this existence by music, which she performs upon the *dole* [ḍhol] or the *tom-tom* [ḍholak] accompanied by her voice". Again, in describing women of rank and wealth (II.3.2), he writes that "the utmost extent of their refinement in the pleasing arts is to play on a *tom-tom*, an instrument on which they sometimes attain some degree of perfection".

Sukumar Ray, writing of the folk music of Bengal, notes that the ḍhol "was taken up by the people of upper society in Calcutta",[6] and that "connoisseurs of music used to take a fancy to expert DHOL-playing in their parlours".[7]

NOTES

1 Dick and Dournon, "Ḍhol", NGMI, 1: 560-62. Also see Ray, *Folk-Music of Eastern India*, 42.
2 Musiciologist Deben Bhattacharya notes that in playing the ḍhol, the drummer uses a friction or scraping technique with the stick. Letter to the author, 17 February, 1992.
3 Dick and Dournon, "Ḍhol", 561. Also see Dick, "Paṭaha", NGMI, 3: 21-22.
4 Solvyns portrays the chewing of pān in III.11.6.
5 678.
6 *Folk-Music of Eastern India*, 42.
7 *Music of Eastern India*, 105.

15. Khol[1]

Calcutta: Sec. XI, No. 10. A Khole or Mirden,—the Tube of the Drum is of earthen ware.
Paris: II.8.4. Khole or Mirden.

Although many people look upon this instrument as sacred, and that it is often seen, especially in their religious festivals, in the hands of the devout Hindoos, such as Faquirs[2] and Beeshnubs [Baiṣṇab], it is not less true that the people make use of it also at their feasts. The form of the *Khole* is exactly such as I have represented it in this engraving; it is sufficient to look at it, to have a perfect idea of this instrument, which consists meerly in a piece of earthen ware covered at the two ends with a skin stretched like our drums, except that the lower end is wider and produces a deeper sound than the upper. It is not necessary to remark that the music of the *Khole* is as monotonous as that of the other instruments which I have been describing. But the Hindoos, on the contrary, find in it an extraordinary charm, and pretend that, accompanied by the voice, this instrument is capable of expressing all the emotions of the soul, from the most violent to the most tender.

At their great festivals a number of these *Kholes* are generally seen contending with each other in noise and uproar. (See numbers 2 and 3 of the first vol.)[3] I have been assured that, in former times, all Hindous were not indiscriminately allowed to play upon it, and even now those who make most use of it are, as I have already mentioned, almost always of the devout class.

The accessories of the print represent, as in all the other plates of Hindoo instruments, the places in which they are generally heard.

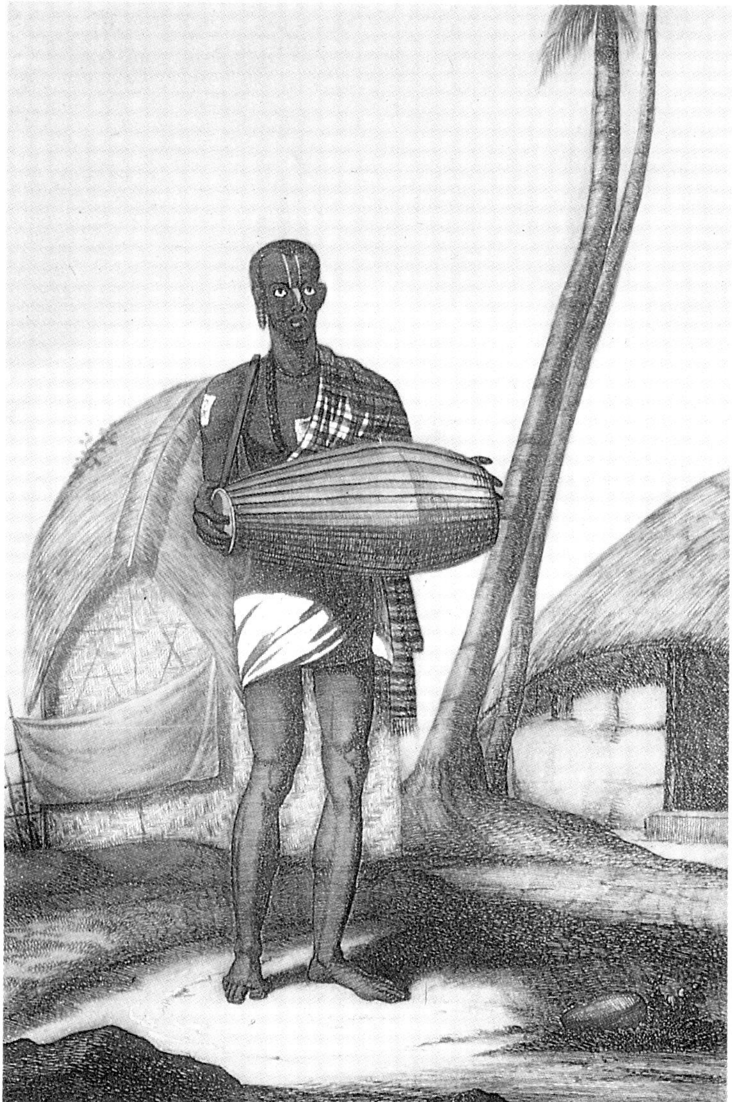

KHOL. Paris II.8.4.

COMMENTARY

The khol is a classical Indian double-headed drum of eastern India. The body is made from clay in an asymmetrical barrel shape. The tapering toward the right end of the khol's body is more sharply accentuated than that of the classical pakhāvaj associated with the *dhrupad* tradition of north Indian music. Like the pakhāvaj, the khol has a treble right head tuned to a specific pitch and a lower-pitched bass left head. However, the khol is tuned higher than the pakhāvaj and has a metallic timbre.

The khol is closely associated with *kīrtan* (devotional singing) of the Vaiṣṇava tradition of Śrī Caitanya Mahāprabhū, the late sixteenth century *bhakti* poet-saint of Bengal. The instrument continues to be looked upon as sacred by Vaiṣṇava devotees of this sect, and its worship, along with that of the kartāl cymbals, still forms part of the ritual practices of the *kīrtan* event. Solvyns depicts the use of the khol—which he refers to as "mirdun" (mṛdaṅga)—along with the bā̃k and kartāl in his portrayal of Hari Saṅkīrtan, a congregational singing of devotional songs praising Hari (an epithet of Viṣṇu).[4] The practice is believed to have been begun by Caitanya.

The "Beeshnubs" (Baiṣṇabs) mentioned by Solvyns are Vaiṣṇava. Solvyns portrays a Baiṣṇab in one of etchings depicting Hindu ascetics, and writes that they are "individuals who, after having renounced all the pleasures of life, the riches and good things of the earth, devote themselves to the worship of Vishnou".[5] The figure depicted in the etching wears the mark of Viṣṇu on his forehead. The "faquirs" mentioned might have been Bauls, who are known to have adopted the khol from the Vaiṣṇava tradition.[6]

The khol is used in religious contexts of sects other than the Caitanya Vaiṣṇava now as it was in Solvyns's time. In discussing "Rhaumien-Gauyin" (Rāmāyan Gāyan), singing the exploits of Rāmā, Solvyns notes that the recital is generally accompanied by such musical instruments as mṛdaṅga, khol, and kartāl.[7] Here he seems to distinguish the khol and mṛdaṅga, but in the title to the khol etching, Solvyns gives its name as "Khole or Mirden", and from his Hari Saṅkīrtan, the two names would seem to refer to the same instrument. Sukumar Ray, in *Folk-Music of Eastern India*, writes that the khol is often called the "*Mridanga* of Bengal",[8] and

Bandyopadhyaya, in *Musical Instruments of India*, says that the khol, widely used in Bengal, is also known as "mṛdaṅga".[9] The mṛdaṅga (meaning "clay-bodied") was the ancient clay drum of the *dhrupad* singers, who replaced it with the wooden barrel pakhāvaj (II.9.4).

NOTES

1 Dick, "Khol", NGMI, 2: 423-24. Also see Ray, *Folk-Music of Eastern India*, 42-43.
2 Solvyns uses the term *faquir* (fakir) to refer to Hindu religious ascetics and mendicants.
3 Solvyns refers to plates I.2.1, Rāmāyan Gāyan, and I.3.1, Hari Saṅkīrtan.
4 I.3.1.
5 II.4.5.
6 Capwell, 108.
7 I.2.1.
8 42.
9 71. It should be noted that the Bengali mṛdaṅga differs from the South Indian mṛdaṅgam both in shape and sound.

16. Ḍholak[1]

Calcutta: Sec. XI, No. 18. A D'holuk,—small drum.
Orme: 53.
Paris: II.8.5. D'Holuk.

Simply to say that the *D'Holuk* is also called *Tomtom,* is giving a very true idea of a sound of this instrument, which may be looked upon as national in Hindoostan; for, of all their musical instruments, this is the most common as well among the natives as among the Mussulmen, the Armenians, the Portugese, and other foreigners. The *Tomtom* is to be met with in every house and in every body's hands: it is the amusement and delight of them all, men and women, young and old. The *D'Holuk* is also a sort of drum, as the print represents it: the manner of playing upon it is as simple as its form; nothing more is required than to strike with the fingers the two skins which cover the ends of the wood, one of which, being less than the other, gives a sharper sound. Although an European finds this music very monotonous, the Hindoos nevertheless have various means of varying the tone of it by the different degrees of force with which they strike it. There are some who play it with astonishing rapidity. The public women and kept mistresses are never without a *Tomtom,* with which they endeavour to relieve the langour and insipidity of their unhappy situation, using it sometimes to accompany their voice, which has frequently a very pleasing effect.

The music of the *D'Holuk* not being loud, it is seldomer found in the open air than in their houses, where good players are sometimes heard with great pleasure.

DHOLAK. Paris II.8.5.

Commentary

As noted in discussion of the ḍhol, Solvyns reversed the labelling on the two prints in the Paris edition. Here, correctly depicted as in the Calcutta edition, the ḍholak is portrayed as normally played, only by the hands. Known to have been an instrument of the Mughal courts, the ḍholak was by Solvyns's time, as it remains today, common throughout North India and played by members of all classes of society. It is apparent that the practice of modulating the pitch of the bass head by sliding either the thumb or the heel of the left hand along the skin, as is also done on the modern tablā, was a ḍholak technique known to players in the eighteenth century.

The ḍholak is frequently described as a small ḍhol, and in contrast to the ḍhol, this popular instrument is widely used in indoor performance as Solvyns protrays it.

Solvyns describes the ḍholak as a "tomtom", a word sometimes used generically for a small drum and, in the quaint phrasing of the *Oxford English Dictionary*, "extended to the drums of barbarous people generally". *Hobson-Jobson* gives the origin as Hindustani *ṭamṭam*, an onomatopoeia for the beat of the drum.[2] Whitworth, in his *Anglo-Indian Dictionary*, gives the Bengali form as *ṭanṭan*, "a small drum".[3]

NOTES

1 Dick, Babiracki, and Webber, "Ḍholak", NGMI, 1: 562-63. Variants: ḍholki, ḍhulkī, ḍōlak, ḍulki.

2 929-30.

3 320.

17. Tablā[1]

Calcutta: Sec. XI, No. 17. A Tubla,—wooden Drums.
Orme: 52.
Paris: II.8.6. Tubla.

The *Tubla* is composed of two tymbals, one of earthen ware, the other of wood, both of them covered with a skin upon which the musician strikes with his fingers. Each tymbal gives a different sound, the mixture of which produces tolerable music. The engraving shews the attitude of the performer and the manner of treating the instrument.

I have already more than once observed that the amusements of the Hindoos are adapted to the manners and way of living of the different classes: the better sort are distinguished, even in their modes of diversion, from those who are without principles of honour. Several musical instruments are in use only among this latter sort: of this number is the *Tubla,* which in general is played only by *Loutchias,*[2] people of dissolute manners, and by public prostitutes, who have it played in their houses by those who frequent them and share in their debaucheries. The dress of the musician represented in the engraving, differs from the national costume of the Hindoos, because men of this class, in contempt of the laws of their country, affect in their appearance a resemblance with the Mussulmen. He is seated on a carpet or piece of cotton cloth. A wooden box, a pitcher, a candlestick with a *charrack,*[3] or a little lamp, forms the whole of his household furniture. In the background is another musician carrying a *Sarinda.*

TABLA. Paris II.8.6.

COMMENTARY

The assertion that the tablā was played only by "loutchias" is probably incorrect. Willard describes the tablā as an instrument of great popularity at the court of the Nawab of Banda, and it can be assumed that the instrument was part of the instrumentarium at other Mughal courts. It is notable that the musician pictured is holding the tablā in the same manner as is done in *qawwālī* ensembles,[4] with the bass drum (*bāyā̃*) in the lap of the performer. The right hand's position is the same as in modern tablā performance.

Earthenware *bāyā̃* continue to be made, especially for beginning students. Metal *bāyā̃* were not necessarily unknown in Solvyns's time. Copper bāyā̃ are mentioned by writers in the late nineteenth century,[5] and wooden ones are not unknown even today.

Risley writes that "The tablā-wala, or drum-maker, is always a Muchi [Mucī]", the Bengali leather-working caste. "Goats' skins are used for the covering, while cows' hides supply the strings for tightening the parchment. On every native drum, at one or both ends, black circles (*khiran*) are painted to improve the pitch. The Muchi prepares a paste of iron filings and rice, with which he stains the parchment." Risley also notes that "At all Hindu weddings, they [Mucīs] are employed as musicians, and engaged in bands, along with Muhamadans."[6]

NOTES

1 Dick and Sen, "Tablā", NGMI, 3: 492-97. Variant: ṭabla.
2 For a discussion of "loutchia", see commentary under Sitār, Pl. 8.
3 What Solvyns refers to here is unclear. The Anglo-Indian *charrack*, a corruption of the Persian *charkh*, is the word for wheel.
4 Qawwālī are the songs of the Muslim sūfī assembly.
5 See, for example, French, "Catalogue of Indian Musical Instruments", in Tagore, 261, and Day, 138.
6 Risley, 2: 99. See Solvyns, Mucī, I.12.3. For a discussion of the Mucī as musician, see commentary under Joorghaje, Pl. 18.

18. Joorghaje

Calcutta: Sec. XI, No. 24. A Joorg-haje,—two Drums of different sizes.
Paris: II.9.2. Joorghaje, a musical instrument.

Although we have already seen a variety of musical instruments in the foregoing numbers, there remains a still greater number to be described in the remainder of this and the following, which are to complete the second volume. It is, as we must have already remarked, their most noisy instruments that the Hindoos have endeavoured to vary. Noise being always more pleasing to their ears than harmony, of which they are very little sensible, or have rather no idea whatsoever, they have been studious to encrease the pleasures suited to their taste, by giving to their music at least the charm of variety. The merit of invention is not what is most striking in the construction of these instruments; but still we cannot help being surprised that a people so evidently without the genius of music, should have been so anxious to multiply the means of this amusement, and have carried the number of their instruments much beyond what we have done in Europe.

I have already represented many which bear a strong resemblance to our drums, and are used to beat the time and mark the cadence and movement of the steps in their religious processions and feasts. This is the use they make of the *Joorghaje* which this print represents: this instrument consists of two long cases of an unequal size, the skin on the under part is beaten with the fingers, that on the upper side with a stick: the sounds follow sometimes in a quicker, sometimes in a slower measure, as in the other instruments. The performers are generally men of the lowest classes, *Doams* [Dom] or *Moochees* [Mucī].

JOORGHAJE. Paris II.9.2.

Commentary

The name seems to indicate a pair (*joṛ*) of *ghaje*—Hindi for "elephant". Drums having names sounding similar to *ghaje* exist in eastern India. The ghasā is a barrel drum with raised hoops that is struck on one side with a cane and rubbed on the other side with a crook-stick. It is played by the Pana musicians of southern Orissa. Dick relates this to the medieval ghaḍasa, a barrel drum played partly by friction.[1] A drum pair of similar construction to this joorghaje is the pambai of South India.[2] It is not possible, however, to establish a connection between the joorghaje and any of these other instruments on the basis of Solvyns's description.

Of the Doms,[3] also known as Caṇḍal, *Hobson-Jobson* describes them as "a very low caste. . . . In many places they perform such offices as carrying dead bodies, removing carrion, & *c.* They are often musicians. . . ."[4] Risley identifies them as in charge of the burning *ghāṭs* at Banaras and associated generally with the disposal of the dead. But, while a degraded position is forced upon all Dom by reason of this role, most Dom, Risley states, follow "the comparatively clean occupation of making baskets and mats".[5] Risley cites Carnegy, *Notes on the Races of Avadh (Oudh)*, that "it is not uncommon for men of this class to rise to high office under kings by whom they were employed as musicians".[6] In Bengal, Risley writes, "the Bajunia [Dom] subcaste are employed to make highly discordant music at marriages and festivals. His women-folk, however, only perform as musicians at the weddings of their own people, it being considered highly derogatory for them to do so for outsiders."[7]

The Mucī[8] are variously identified as a branch of or identical with Chamār caste. Mucī are the leather workers of Bengal, engaged as "tanners, shoe-makers, saddlers, musicians, and basket-makers".[9] "At all Hindu weddings they are employed as musicians, and engaged in bands, as among Muhamadans. Their favourite instruments are drums of various shapes and sizes, the violin, and the pipe."[10] Jogendra Nath Bhattacharya states that "for the Muchi and Mohamedan musicians who are a necessity on festive occasions, there is generally special accommodation in the mansions of the rich and in the big temples. . . . [T]he Muchi bands entertain the bye-standers from the Nat-Mandir or dancing hall in front of the puja *dalan* or chapel."[11]

NOTES

1 Dick, "Ghaḍasa", NGMI, 2: 39.
2 Deva, 85.
3 Solvyns, I.11.6.
4 322.
5 1: 249.
6 1: 240.
7 1: 250.
8 Solvyns, I.12.3.
9 Risley, 2: 98.
10 Ibid., 2: 99.
11 213.

19. Ṭikārā[1]

Calcutta: Sec. XI, No. 31. A Tickora,—played at Nautches, Feasts, &c. Paris: II.9.3. Tichora, a musical instrument.

Here is another instrument of the same nature as the foregoing, as well in its form as in the manner of playing upon it. The *Tichora,* as is shown in the print, is also composed of two tymbals, one of which is rather smaller than the other. The performer is generally seated on the ground behind his instrument; but in the public ceremonies, marriages, cavalcades of persons of high rank, or on the arrival of a Radjah [rājā], the instrument is carried on the camels of the retinue, where the *Tichora* becomes a mark of honor, and adds to the solemnity of the feast or procession. It will easily be perceived that I could not represent this ceremony without losing the exact form of the instrument which I wished to give: for this reason I have preferred a drawing of a performer on the *Tichora* sitting before the house of a person who, according to the Hindoo custom, hires musicians with the permission of the *Jemindar* [*zamīndār*][2] of the district. Although the *Tichora* is originally of Hindoostan, it is seldom played but by Mussulmen. At the Radjahs nevertheless and in the Nautches, it is sometimes used by Hindoos of inferior casts, but not so low as the tanners, nightmen, or undertakers.

Commentary

According to Dick, the ṭikārā of Bengal is a single kettledrum, while that of Orissa is a "paired, earthenware kettledrum with the skins braced with ropes and tuning paste applied to the lower drum".[3] Solvyns, however, depicts the instrument as paired

ṬIKĀRĀ. Paris II.9.3.

kettledrums. Shoberl, in his description of the "tikora", follows Solvyns, and adds that it is frequently seen in the train of Mārāṭha, carried on a camel that follows the elephant upon which the prince rides.[4] But Shoberl also describes a "double drum, used on occasion of festivals and processions" as a "nagur".[5] The ceremonial use of the instrument described by Solvyns and its use primarily by Muslim performers would seem to indicate that the drums referred to were what would be most widely recognized as nagāṛā (Pl. 21).

NOTES

1 Dick, "Ṭikārā", NGMI, 3: 584.
2 See commentary on Ḍhāk, Pl. 13.
3 Dick, "Ṭikārā", NGMI, 3: 584.
4 3: 20.
5 3: 21.

20. Pakhāvaj[1]

Calcutta: Sec. XI, No. 32. A Pukwauz,—used as the foregoing [i.e. at Nautches, Feasts, &c.]
Orme: 58.
Paris: II.9.4. Pucwauz.

Those who remember my former description of the *Khole* will find some resemblance between that instrument and the *Pucwauz* which this plate represents: but it must be observed, that it is not like it made of baked earth, but of wood covered at the two ends with a skin; little bits of wood moveable at pleasure at one of the ends join these skins together. The *Pucwauz* is seldom heard at the feasts or ceremonies of religion, but is in frequent use at private entertainments, especially in Nautches, where it often serves for accompanying. On these occasions performers rather of an higher cast are hired. It is also an amusement for several casts of Hindoos, who play upon it for hours together in their houses, and appear exceedingly delighted with the sounds which they produce by striking the skins in a variety of motion with their hands. The Hindoo in the print is an inhabitant of the country, seated before his house, and giving himself up to the enjoyment of the freshness of the air and the sounds of his instrument. He is drest in blue and white cloth, which shews that he is of the northern parts of Hindoostan, or that he follows the doctrine of *Bichno* [Viṣṇu], whose sectaries affect those colours.

COMMENTARY

The pakhāvaj, also called mṛdaṅg, is known today as the primary percussion accompaniment in musical genres belonging to the *dhrupad* style. In previous times it was associated with some

PAKHĀVAJ. Paris II.9.4.

traditions of *kīrtan* singing, especially that of the Vallabhā *Sampradāya,* a Vaiṣṇava sect of western India, and with court dance. It is the most classical of the North Indian drums and apparently has enjoyed such high esteem throughout its long history that it has been acceptable for use by members of the highest Hindu castes. Exponents of the pakhāvaj have steadily decreased in number with the decline of the *dhrupad* tradition, beginning in the eighteenth century. The resurgence of interest in *dhrupad* singing during the last two decades has helped to promote the rediscovery of the pakhāvaj, but has not yet secured the survival of the tradition.

NOTE

See discussion of the "northern mṛdaṅg or pakhāvaj" by Dick in "Mṛdaṅga", NGMI, 2: 696-99; and Bandyopadhyaya, "Pakhāwaja", 72-74. The Bengali form is pākhwāj.

21. Nagāṛā[1]

Calcutta: Sec. XI, No. 27. A Nagra,—played on by two sticks.
Orme: 56.
Paris: II.9.5. NAGRA.

This print represents one of those couriers who in India perform the functions of the postrunning on foot, from town to town, with letters and commissions in a leather sack. They are called *Dauks* [*dāk*] in the Hindoo language, and are remarkable for their fidelity and extraordinary dispatch.

The reader will not immediately perceive how these circumstances are connected with the musical instrument which I am going to describe. It is necessary then to inform him that it is confirmed by long experience, that the sound of the *Nagra* has the effect of driving away the dangerous animals, such as tygers and serpents, which, to the great terror of the traveller, infest the high roads of Hindoostan. As the instrument, which resembles a small drum, is very portable, all those who have to traverse any unfrequented country are preceded by a *Kouli* [*kulī*, or coolie] constantly beating the *Nagra,* whether they travel in a palanquin or on foot. Even servants have a *Nagra*-beater to accompany them when they are sent on commissions by their masters to any distance. The couriers or *Dauks* have always one before them, which they transmit with their packets to those of the next station, who forward them as rapidly and in the same manner. During the night they have besides two *Koulies* with *machals* [*masal*] or torches to light them.

So simple is the mode of communication among the Hindoos, As to the *Nagra,* to which sometime the *Kaura* is added, I have given a sufficient idea of this noisy instrument by describing its

NAGĀṘĀ. Paris II.9.5.

use. I have only to add that it is also heard at public festivals and in all great ceremonies.

COMMENTARY

The shape of the instrument in Solvyns's portrait is obscured by a decorative skirt. Nagāṛā generally refers to kettledrum in South Asia. Its uses have been diverse, ranging from an instrument of the court, shrine or temple ceremonial band (*naubat*) to an accompanying instrument for tribal dances in eastern Bihar and Bengal. Modern writers do not mention use of the nagāṛā as a noise-making device to drive away wild animals, but the use of the drums is still a part of game hunting in India. The *dākwālā* (postman) or *kulī* (hired laborer or burden-carrier) no longer beats nagāṛā in the context of their occupations.

The figure Solvyns's depicts is a *dāk*, or mail carrier. The term *dāk* (Anglo-Indian, *dawk* or *dauk*) was used both for post and postman, but its more precise and broader meaning refers to transport by relays of men and horses, stationed at intervals—an institution in India dating at least from the fourteenth century. As well as for the post, a relay system was used for carrying passengers in palanquins.[2]

In British India, a postal system, apparently introduced by Clive in 1766,[3] used the *dāk*. As Lady Nugent described it in her Calcutta journal in 1814, "There are three men; one carries the bangy, or basket, which holds the letters—I should say rather, baskets for there is one for letters and another for packages—these are equally balanced, and swung, by a light bamboo, over the man's shoulders. The other carries a torch, for they always set off at night, and travel night and day. The third man has a tomtom [Solvyns's nagāṛā] on which he beats incessantly, to keep off tigers and other wild beasts. They all three run very fast, keeping close to each other, for the light is as necessary as the music, and the dauk, or postman, is always between the two others."[4]

In his ethnographic notes of 1883 on Eastern Bengal, Wise writes that "Formerly the naqārah [nagāṛā] players were Chamārs [leather workers], but of late years the lower grade of

Muhammadans . . . are exclusively employed, and are known as Bājunia."[5]

NOTES

1 Dick and Babiracki, "Nagāṙā", NGMI, 2: 739-41. Variants: nagārā, nagaṙa, naqqāra, naghāṙā, etc.
2 "Dawk" in *Hobson-Jobson*, 299-300; "dak" in *Oxford English Dictionary*.
3 Ivie, 130-31, cited in Nair, ed., *British Social Life in Ancient Calcutta (1750-1850)*, 46-47.
4 2: 254, quoted in Nair, *Calcutta in the 19th Century*, 171-72.
5 Entry under "Bajhunia", 39. Wise notes that a nagāṙā band "plays at each 'pahar', or watch of the day".

22. Kāṛā[1]

Calcutta: Sec. XI, No. 28. A Kaura,—beaten with a stick.
Orme: 57.
Paris: II.9.6. Kaura.

The only difference between this instrument and the *Nagra* represented in the preceding print is, that the former is beaten with one stick only, whereas two are used for this. The feathers and tassels which surround this sort of drum are merely ornaments with which the Hindoos are fond of decorating every object of luxury or festivity. Besides its use on journeys, which I have noticed in speaking of the *Nagra,* this instrument serves also in opulent houses to announce the arrival of ceremonious visitors. Among people of distinction *Kauras* are placed at certain distances, from the entrance to the audience chamber. He who is nearest to the first door proclaims the arrival of strangers by a signal, and pronounces their names in a loud voice. A *Kaura* is always seen hanging at the door of great houses with the bucklers of the *Chokidars* [*caukīdār*] or guards, of whom we have spoken in the first volume.[2]

It is also with the sound of the *Kaura* that the *bazars* or markets are opened. The *Jemindar* [*zamīndār*][3] of the district makes known by this signal that every Hindoo may bring his wares for sale, and find safety and protection for his goods and person while the market lasts.

Commentary

Solvyns once again provides a contradiction between what is described and depicted. The nagāṛā is shown being played with two sticks and the kāṛā with one, yet he states that the main

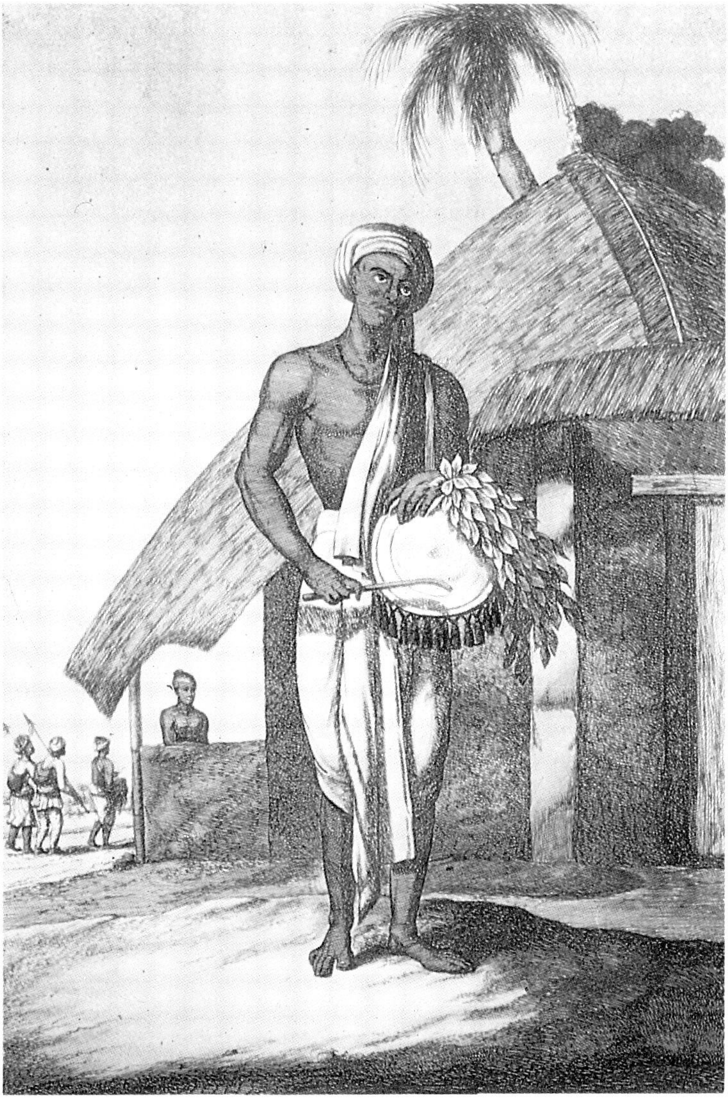

KĀṘĀ. Paris II.9.6.

distinction between the two drums is that the former is played with one stick and the latter with two. It seems likely that Solvyns intended to emphasize that the nagāṛā is played with two sticks, as he notes in the 1799 *Catalogue*, but here inadvertently reversed his reference.

Dick states that the kāṛā is similar to the smaller ṭikārā kettledrum of Bengal.[4] Babiraki, however, describes the karah as a "double-headed drum with a truncated-conical wooden body and laced-on skin heads" of Bengal. The term also occurs among tribal groups of southern Bihar in reference to a specific function (filling in syncopated patterns with even groups of beats and rolls) provided by a member of the percussion section in an instrumental ensemble.[5]

From Solvyns we learn that several musical instruments fulfilled conventional functions in the zamīndār society of Bengal in the eighteenth century that were apparently lost with the implementation of land reform.

NOTES

1 Dick, "Kāṛā", NGMI, 3: 360. Babiracki, NGMI, 2: 360, describes the "Karah", a distinct instrument with a similar name.

2 The specific reference to Vol. I is unclear, and perhaps Solvyns refers to the Brajbāsī guard (I.8.4). For caukīdār, see IV.4.6.

3 Landholder. See commentary on Dhāk, Pl. 13.

4 Solvyns's Ṭikārā (Pl. 19). See Dick, "Ṭikārā", NGMI, 3: 584.

5 Babiracki, "Karah", NGMI, 2: 360.

23. Ḍamphā[1]

Calcutta: Sec. XI, No. 12. A Dump. Species of Tabors.
Paris: II.10.2. Dump.

The instruments which I am going to describe in this number are common only in certain parts of Hindoostan, and are scarcely known in others. That which is represented in this print, called *Dump,* is a large drum differing from ours, only in its octagon form and its being beaten only with the right hand; whence it may be supposed that it can serve but to accompany a band, and is therefore must used in religious festivals. The dress of the musician is not bengale. The cottage which he inhabits is seen in the background; it is composed of bambous and mats. This is the most general mode of construction in the north of Hindoostan, where the earth has not sufficient consistence to be employed in raising cabins. It is near a stream, for the Hindoos always seek the vicinity of water for their dwelling. The country, of which a part is seen, represents the mountainous parts of Hindoostan.

Commentary

The ḍamphā of Bengal is an octagonal frame drum belonging to a class of drums most widely known in India as ḍaph. Although frame drums existed in India before the Muslim invasions, as evidenced in sculpture, ḍaph drums, including the ḍamphā and the doira of the following print (Pl. 24), were introduced into northern India from the Middle East in the twelfth century.[2] With the exception of the South Indian kanjira, frame drums are to be found today primarily among folk and tribal cultures in South Asia.

ḌAMPHĀ. Paris II.10.2.

The ḍaph is played typically with the fingers of the right hand, while intermittent strokes are executed with a stick held in the left forefinger and manipulated by the middle finger. As Solvyns portrays the ḍamphā and notes in the text, however, the player supports the base of the instrument with his left hand and beats the drum with his right hand. Dick states that "This type [of ḍaph] has earlier been recorded for other parts of India under the name *ḍamphā* (e.g., in Bengal, where it is hand-played), but does not appear common nowadays."[3] According to Solvyns's description, the ḍamphā was not common in Bengal, although S. Bandyopadhyaya, in *Musical Instruments of India,* with particular focus on Bengal, writes that it is played on various festivals and processions and invariably at Holi[4]—and Solvyns himself prominently portrays it in his depiction of the Dol Yātrā, as Holi is celebrated in Bengal.[5]

The octagonal variety of frame drum portrayed by Solvyns is known in Rajasthan today as the gherā (a term that, paradoxically, derives from a word meaning "circular").[6]

Solvyns's reference to the mountainous part of the country is unclear, for it is not depicted in the print.

NOTES

1 "Ḍamphā", NGMI, 1: 540; Dick, "Ḍaph", NGMI, 1: 545-46.
2 Dick, "Ḍaph", NGMI, 1: 545.
3 Ibid.
4 77-78.
5 I.8.1.
6 Dick, "Ḍaph", NGMI, 1: 545.

24. Doira[1]

Calcutta: Sec. XI, No. 13. A Doyra. Species of Tabors.
Paris: II.10.3. Doyra.

It would be a great mistake for Europeans who have resided at Calcutta, or in the other towns of Bengal, to pretend that the *Doyra* is not an Hindoo instrument, because they have never heard it played. For, notwithstanding the *Doyra* is not used in Bengal, it has nevertheless been known for time immemorial in different parts of India. In general, many of the customs which are the subject of this work may appear foreign, without affording any reason to infer from thence, that they do not belong to the Hindoos; for, what is well-known in one province, is frequently unknown in another at a very small distance from it. To bring together and describe all these different customs, is the chief aim of this collection, and I hope that I have not omitted anything which relates to the Hindoo nation.

The *Doyra* is an instrument like our tambourine, surrounded with copper rings which the musician shakes with one hand, while he strikes with the other the interior skin. There is nothing particular in the manner of playing it.

Commentary

Contrary to Solvyns's assertion, this type of frame drum, belonging to the ḍaph class, most probably entered India with the Muslims beginning in the twelfth century. The name for the drum in India, *doira,* and its many variants, comes from the Persian *dāirā* ("circle"), and the drum itself is related to the Arabic duff.[2] Similar drums with related names are to be found throughout

DOIRA. Paris II.10.3.

West Asia and south-eastern Europe and are, of course, familiar (as Solvyns recognizes) as a tambourine.

NOTES

1 Atanassov, "Daire", NGMI, 1: 536. Variants: dahare, dahira, daira, da'ira, dāirā, dairea, dajre, dāra, dara, dāyre, ghēra, and (used by Solvyns) doira.

2 Ibid. Also see Dick, "Ḍaph", NGMI, 1: 545-46.

25. Jagajhampa

Calcutta: Sec. XI, No. 33. A Jugo, Jhumpo,—one side is beaten while the other is rubbed.
Orme: 59.
Paris: II.10.4. Jugo, Jhumpo.

This instrument is still less known than the two former, and I have remarked that the Hindoos themselves, when they have heard it played, have asked with surprise whence the music came that was so foreign to their ears. As the Hindoos never travel, we must not be surprised at their admiration of everything which comes from a country beyond that where they were born. The sound of this instrument has moreover something particular in it. It is a humming sound produced by rubbing a long stick at the end of which is a clew of packthread upon a skin stretched over a cylinder of earthen ware. This cylinder is composed of two parts which join and are covered over with a skin which may be loosened or made tighter at pleasure, by means of a band which goes round the instrument. The musician, at the same time that he draws his long stick over one of the skins, strikes it with a second stick which he holds with his other hand.

Commentary

A search of available literature on Indian music failed to yield these terms or the exact instrument witnessed by Solvyns, although in rural areas of Bengal and Bangladesh, the instrument portrayed is still known as either jugojhamp or jugol.[1] Sen's *An Etymological Dictionary of Bengali* gives "jagajhampa" as "a kind of drum and drum beating"; the first element, *jaga*, is onomatopoeic, and the second, *jhampa*, means to leap or jump.[2] The word *jagajhampa*

JAGAJHAMPA. Paris II.10.4.

perhaps from the sound of the drum, means "cacophony" in modern Bengali.

T.C. Gupta, in *Aspects of Bengali Society*, describes the jagajhampa as a kind of kettle-drum "which is suspended with a cord from the neck of the man who played on it with a pair of cane-sticks. Feathers of birds were used to decorate [it]."[3] But the instrument Solvyns portrays is no kettle-drum, and what Gupta describes fits Solvyns's nagāṙā.

The earthenware body of the jagajhampa and the suggestion of a waisted cylindrical structure that is presented by the portrait indicate that this drum might be a form of the mā̃dar of eastern India. The mā̃dar exists in various forms, but most of these have a baked clay body resembling the waisted cylindrical form of the jagajhampa. The friction technique of playing described by Solvyns is not mentioned in descriptions of the mā̃dar[4] and is not common in Indian drumming, but can be found in the playing of the ghasā (ghaḍasa) barrel drum of the Pāṇa musicians of south Orissa.[5]

According to Deben Bhattacharya, this scraping technique is also used for the Bengali ḍhol. He notes, as well, the similarity of the drum Solvyns depicts to the timila from Kerala.[6] He writes that "although the 'timila' is shaped from wood and is played by hands, it too employs the 'ghasā' or the rubbing technique along with squeezing the waist strap of the drum for pitch variations". Bhattacharya suggests that the jagajhampa may have been played by a similar technique, combining varied sounds produced by beating the drumhead, scraping the skin, and by varying the pitch by tightening and loosening the skin strap placed on the waisted center of the drum.[7]

NOTES

1 As related by Bengali students at the University of Texas at Austin.
2 306.
3 81. Gupta says that it is a favorite instrument of Muslims.
4 See, for example, Babiracki, "Mā̃dar", NGMI, 2: 590-91.
5 Dick, "Ghaḍasa", NGMI, 2: 39.
6 Pitoëss, "Timila", NGMI, 3: 586.
7 Deben Bhattacharya, letter to the author, 17 February 1992.

26. Surmaṇḍal[1]

Calcutta: Sec. XI, No. 34. A Surmungla,—formed of reeds and played on by the hand.
Orme: 60.
Paris: II.10.5. Surmungla.

It will be remarked without difficulty that this instrument is of true Hindoo origin, and that it could have been invented no where but in India; and in reality it is one of the most singular which we have as yet had to describe. The sound of the *Surmungla* is very sweet and grateful to the ear, and produces altogether a very good effect; and yet of what does the music of this instrument consist? The musician does no more than pass his fingers over some pieces of bambou split at the two ends, and kept together by thin traverses: all the rest is represented in the print.

An European cannot help being surprised at hearing such sweet sounds from so simple an instrument; he never could have thought that so much could be made of it.

The *Surmungla* is little known in the flat countries, but it is in great repute in the mountainous parts of Hindoostan. At Calcutta it is seen only among traders, and sometimes with palanquin bearers and other servants, who come originally from the mountains.

The performer here represented is surrounded by a crowd of curious people who are listening to him with great attention, and are never tired of this music.

COMMENTARY

The instrument pictured appears to be the idiochord raft zither known as dendung[2] in Assam. It was apparently known in a wider geographical area in the eighteenth century than it is today. The

SURMAṆḌAL. Paris II.10.5.

term surmaṇḍal has been applied since Mughal times to a plucked board zither in North India. Hindu musicologists link the surmaṇḍal to the mattakokilā vīṇā, mentioned in the *saṅgitaratnākara* through later textual references. However, it is more likely that the term was coined to name the Middle Eastern qānūn brought to India by invading Muslim armies and mentioned in court records of the Delhi Sultanate.

Solvyns writes that the musician he portrays is surrounded by listeners, although none is depicted in the etching.

NOTES

1 Dick, "Surmaṇḍal", NGMI, 3: 477. Variant: svaramaṇḍala.

2 Dick, "Dendung", NGMI, 1: 556.

27. Khanjari[1]

Calcutta: Sec. XI, No. 14. A Khunjery. Species of Tabors.
Paris: II.10.6. K'hunjery.

The *K'hunjery*, a sort of little drum, serves to accompany the voice; it is most used by the Faquirs, the *Beeshnubs* [Baiṣṇab][2] and the *Kawns* [Kān], those professional singers of whom I have spoken in the eleventh number of the first volume:[3] this instrument therefore is known in all the countries of Hindoostan.

The musician in the print is an Hindoo whose whole life is spent in singing the praises, the incarnation and the loves of some divinity of the country, going from house to house, and existing upon the alms which he receives. To draw the attention of passengers, and still more to excite their pity, he paints his face, his breast and arms even more than the Faquirs; and while he is playing, makes the most horrible grimaces and contorsions, so as to make it believed that it is not without the greatest pain that he can draw the sounds from his *K'hunjery*.

The background represents some of those buildings which are common in the Indian country.

Commentary

The khanjari is a variety of frame drum, distinguished from other types by its small size and deep, heavy frame. Some are tambourine-like, with metal discs fastened in slots cut into the wooden frame. In Bengal, the head is made from the skin of the iguana; in other parts of the subcontinent, leather or snake skin might be used. According to Deva, crocodile skin or iguana skin is used for the head of the related South Indian kanjira.[4] This variety of the

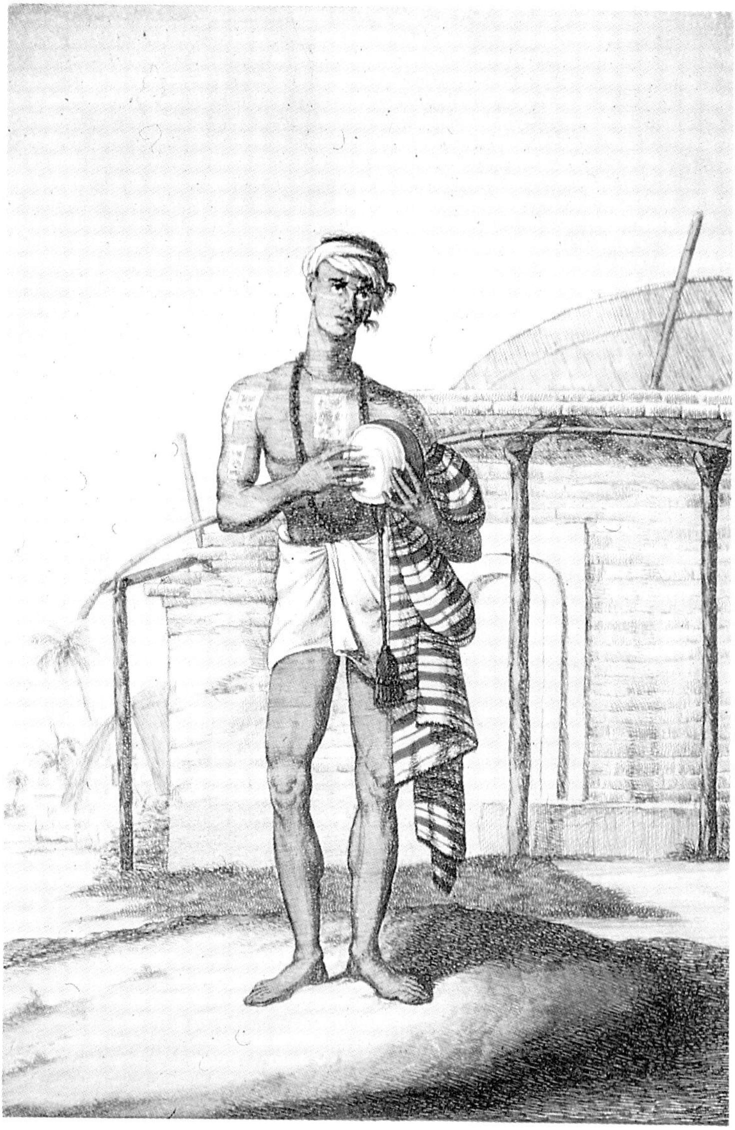

KHANJARI. Paris II.10.6.

drum is smaller than its northern counterparts. There it has long been used in the accompaniment of devotional songs of the *bhajana* tradition. Day mentions that it is also used by "Nautch girls".[5]

Kothari identifies the khanjari as played by snake-charmers, along with the pūngī[6]—Solvyns's "tobrie" (Pl. 36).

The "Kawns" to whom Solvyns refers are the professional singers of the Kān caste, which Risley identifies as "a very low caste of musicians akin to the Doms".[7] Deben Bhattacharya suggests that the word may be a corruption of *gāyan*, meaning singer, particularly the Vaiṣṇava singers who accompany themselves with the khol and khanjari during the *prabhāt pheri*, "the morning circulation", singing songs in praise of Kṛṣṇa from door to door.[8]

Solvyns portrays another Kān, with khanjari, in the series of etching of caste occupations, and there writes,

> the Kawns, men, women, and children, earn their subsistance, and spend their lives singing on the highways or before the doors of houses. They accompany themselves sometimes on the tambourin or with the *khole* . . . , and sing, in a disagreeable tone and in a country jargon which few understand, the loves and exploits of the Gods.
>
> The *Kawns* have some affinity to the Musselmans, but without being confounded with them. Though in their dress and in some other particulars, they differ from the other Hindoos, they never wear feathers nor other ornaments by which the Musselmans are distinguished.
>
> The Hindoos of this class also are but little esteemed, either on account of the great number of dissolute persons among them, or of the intercourse which they keep up with other very inferior casts, such as shoe-makers, basket-makers, etc.[9]

NOTES

1 Dick and Dournon, "Khanjari", NGMI, 2: 422. Variants: khanjani, khāñjarī.
2 See commentary on Khol, Pl. 15.
3 I.11.3.
4 142.
5 Ibid.
6 22. In his portrayal of the Sāmperia snake-catchers (II.8.1), Solvyns depicts their use of the hour-glass drum, huḍuk, rather than the

khanjari. For the huḍuk, see Dick, NGMI: 2: 257-58.

7 1: 396. Sukumar Sen, 137, gives *kān* as "the caste name of professional singers".

8 Letter to the author, 17 February, 1992.

9 I.11.3.

28. Kartāl[1]

Calcutta: Sec. XI, No. 11. Kurtaul or Symbols.
Paris: II.11.2. Kurtaul.

There is nothing to be said upon the form of this instrument. It is easy to see that it is no more than a small tymbal carried in the hand. Its antiquity only entitles it to a place here, as it is one of the earliest instruments which the Hindoos possessed. It appears to have been formerly used in religious ceremonies, as a great number of their ancient idols are represented with it. It is now sometimes seen in the hands of people who affect piety, who sing in the streets and markets, and accompany their voice with the *Kurtaul:* they stop generally before the shops in hopes of obtaining the fruit of their labour.

Many of the Hindoo instruments are not much more deserving of notice than the *Kurtaul;* I shall not have admitted them into my collection, had it not been my intention, as I have already mentioned, to give a complete description of the music of this people.

Commentary

The term *kartāl*—literally handclapping—generally denotes wooden clappers that may or may not incorporate jingles. In Bengal, the term is applied to hand-held cymbals, and they are typically used in conjunction with the khol (Pl. 15) as favored instruments in Vaiṣṇava *kīrtan.*[2]

The kartāl is known elsewhere throughout North India either as manjīrā or, in its larger size, jhānjh.[3] In Bengal, the manjīrā, which Solvyns portrays in another etching (Pl. 31), is smaller and of a somewhat different shape.[4]

KARTĀL. Paris II.11.2.

NOTES

1 Dick, "Kartāl", NGMI, 2: 361-62. Variants: kartāla, kartaḷa, kartār. On the kartāl and idiophonic Indian instruments more generally, see Ray, *Folk-Music of Eastern India*, pp. 44-45.

2 Das Gupta, 85.

3 "Jhānjh", NGMI, 2:328.

4 Ibid. Das Gupta terms it "mandira".

29. Kā̃si[1]

Calcutta: Sec. XI, No. 26. A Kaunsy,—a plate of brass beaten by a stick. Paris: II.11.3. Kaunsy.

No feast is celebrated in Hindoostan without having a *Kaunsy* in the music; and in private entertainments it is also one of the commonest instruments. However poor the Hindoo, the *Kaunsy* must be heard in his house on his wedding day. The sound of it is overcoming, especially when many of them are played together. In rich houses strangers are sometimes announced by the *Kaunsy*: in this case, the stick with which it is beaten is larger.

The performers are persons of the lower casts, such as the musician represented in the print.

Commentary

Solvyns appears to make a distinction between the kā̃sar, the temple gong, and the kā̃si, apparently the same instrument used in a secular context. These instruments have been discussed under kā̃sar (Pl. 4).

NOTE

1 See Dick, "Kā̃sar", NGMI, 2: 362. Variants: kansar, kansi, kā̃sya, and kā̃si (the transliteration of Solvyns's "kaunsy").

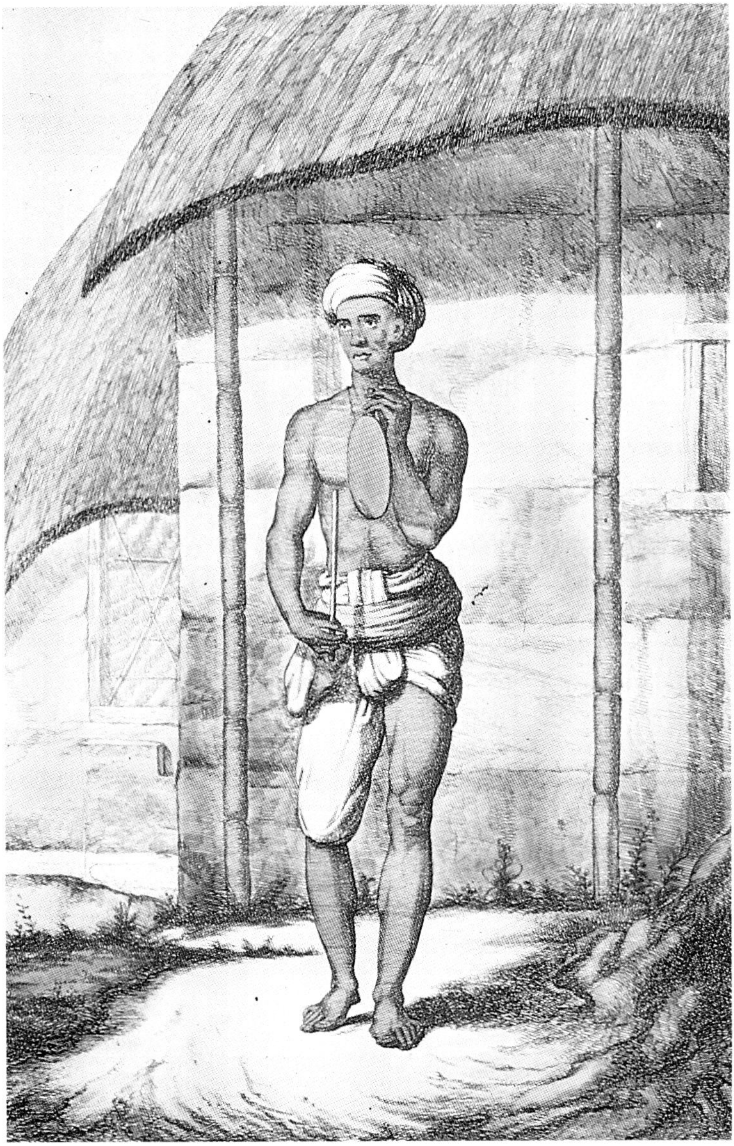

KÃSI. Paris II.11.3.

30. Jaltaraṅg[1]

Calcutta: Sec. XI, No. 19. A Jultrung, earthen or China Cups — fitted to the different notes of music, and played on with two sticks or pieces of iron.
Orme: 54.
Paris: II:11.4. Jultrung.

Though the name of this instrument does not promise much harmony, it produces very agreeable sounds: The *Jultrung* is not unlike the Harmonica, one of our sweetest instruments, but is more simple, consisting meerly in seven *piallas* [*pīelā*, cup] , or earthen vases in a progression of different sizes on the same line, and unequally filled with water, which causes the diversity of tone required. The performer strikes the edges of the vases with a little stick, and draws out a very soft and melodious music. Having remarked that the Hindoos preferred China vases, I asked the reason, but the only answer I could get was that China *piallas* had always been used, though they have in their own country a very fine earth of which they make an excellent ware. The *Jultrung* is not common in Bengal, and is therefore but little known to Europeans. It is to be met with mostly in the northern districts of Hindoostan.

Commentary

The history of the jaltaraṅg is unclear. Textual references to the term do not occur before the seventeenth century, although Bandyopadhyaya, in *Musical Instruments of India,* writes that in the medieval period, metal cups were used for the instrument before the comparatively recent introduction of porcelain cups. He

JALTARAṄG. Paris II.11.4.

gives the literal meaning of the word as "waves of water", and indicates that instead of seven cups, "sixteen to twenty cups are used in its performance to cover a range of two octaves".[2]

Today the instrument is used primarily by Hindustānī musicians, but is not at all common. However, those who do play the jaltaraṅg continue to favor porcelain bowls made in China. The repertory of the jaltaraṅg when played solo is modelled on the *gat* repertory of the sitār and other plucked string instruments. Because of its limited capacity for producing embellishments (*gamak*), the jaltaraṅg is more often used in ensemble performance.

NOTES

1 "Jaltaraṅg", NGMI, 2: 321. Variant: jalataraṅga
2 84-85.

31. Manjīrā[1]

Calcutta: Sec. XI, No. 20. Munjeera,—two brass cups beaten together.
Paris: II.11.5. Munjerrah.

The *Munjeerah* bears some resemblance to our *castagnettes,* but in India the use of it is not confined, as in Europe, to the lower classes; it is the delight of the richer Hindoos. Seated on a carpet with their legs across, whole hours are spent in singing to the sound of their *Munjeerah* an air as monotonous as their music. Such is the occupation of their day, which is interrupted only by smoking and sleeping. Their diet, as I have already observed, is so frugal and simple, that very little time is spent at their meals. The indolence to which they are so entirely given up does not even allow them to seek for any refinement in their pleasures. Repose and idleness are the prerogatives of the Hindoo of rank and fortune. The *Munjeerah* is frequently used in the natches, and is also a favorite instrument of the Hidgras [Hijṛās].[2]

Commentary

In most parts of North India, manjīrā are paired cup cymbals, often joined together by a cord, and distinguished from the kartāl by their smaller size. They are commonly used to keep rhythm in devotional singing, but may also be used to accompany dance or other instruments. A diversity of tones and timbres is obtained from the instrument by striking the two parts together at various angles and through the mixture of damped and non-damped strokes. Small cymbal playing has been developed to virtuoso levels in some areas of India. Deva has written that "the virtuosity sometimes exhibited is really staggering. For instance, the *kamsale*

MANJĪRĀ. Paris II.11.5.

dancers of Mysore form groups of two men, each person holding a pair of small *tala*-s [small cymbals equivalent to manjīrā]. Dancing with exuberance, they clash the cymbals producing rhythmic patterns of great beauty."[3]

NOTES

1 Dick, "Manjīrā", NGMI, 2: 609.

2 As noted in the commentary on the Nautch, Pl. 1, Hijṛās are eunuchs dressed as women who sing and dance in often lewd parody of women. Solvyns portrays them separately, though without reference to music or dance, in II.3.4.

3 55.

32. Jhā̃jhari[1]

Calcutta: Sec. XI, No. 15. A J'haunjree,—two hollow brass rings, containing small Balls, played on by a quick movement of the hand. Paris: II.11.6. J'haunjree.

The *J'haunjree* is also very like our *castagnettes*; it consists of two hollow rings of copper enclosing little balls of the same metal, which the performer puts in motion with his fingers. The pleasure which the Hindoos experience in playing on this little instrument, if it deserves to be called one, is extreme. They appear almost transported with joy at the noise which they produce with their *J'haunjree.*

The accessories of the drawing and the dress of the Hindoo represented, announce a person of a superior cast; though the furniture consists only of a mat that serves as a bed, a box filled with *pawn* [*pān*], the little altars of his domestic gods, and two sticks painted blue and red, fastened to the wall, to hang the clothes upon. All the articles which to us appear indispensible, such as a table, a chair, a bed, are wanting: the Hindoos find it very easy to do without them; and Europeans themselves, after some years residence in India, begin to look upon them as superfluous.

Contrary to the custom of true Hindoos, the man whom I have drawn wears slippers instead of wooden sandals: in this respect his costume differs from that which we have described in the first volume.[2]

Commentary

Carey has defined the term *jhā̃jhari* as "a kind of metal ring with small bells fixed on its periphery, which all ring together when it is properly shaken".[3] An instrument similar to what Solvyns

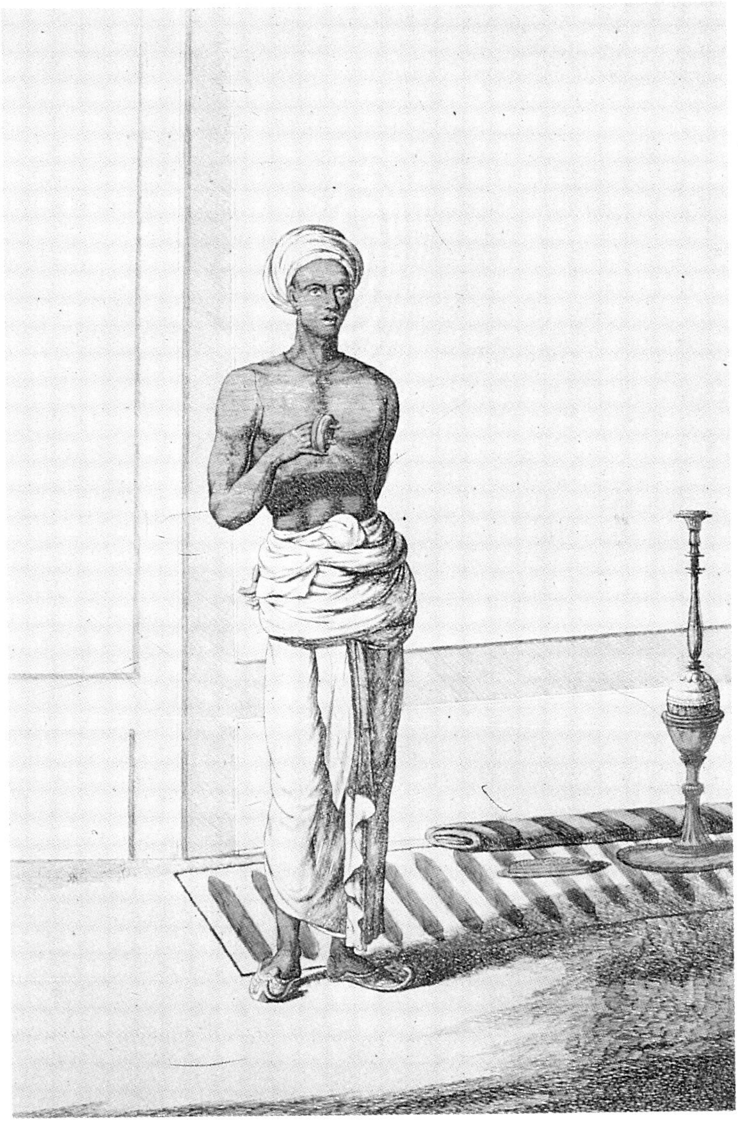

JHĀJHARĪ. Paris II.11.6.

portrays is used today by the Bauls of Bengal. This is the *nūpur*, "a slit tubular anklet filled with shot".[4] However, *nūpur* might also refer to tiny bells attached to decorative jewellery such as anklets (*pāyal*).[5] The term *jhā̃jhari* is onomatopoeic, indicating (from the Bengali) a jingling (*jhā̃j*) cascade (*jharaṇi*). Other instruments of this type in India occur under the names silampu (Tamil Nadu) and gaggara (Karnataka).

NOTES

1 Among variants, Sukumar Sen, 340, gives jhājhuri.
2 In *Les Hindoûs*, Vol. I, Solvyns, in fact, portrays both the kṣatriya (I.2.4) and vaiśya (I.2.5) with slippers and the brahmins bearfoot. He does describe the "remarkable" sandals in I.5.2, where they are worn by a Tā̃ti, or weaver. "They are of wood, and he holds them by a sort of button with his toes. . . ." Solvyns also depicts the wooden sandals in the etching of the kuplyans or bīn, Pl. 6.
3 Carey, 2: 310.
4 Capwell, 100.
5 Deva, 52.

33. Rāmśiṅgā[1]

Calcutta: Sec. XI, No. 30. A Ramsinga,—resembling a Serpent.
Paris: II.12.2. Ramsinga.

We shall conclude in this number the description of the musical instruments; those which remain are wind instruments; the *Ramsinga* is the most remarkable of them. It consists of four pipes of very thin metal which fit one within the other, and are generally covered with a fine red varnish; it is played in the same manner as our large trumpet. It requires very strong lungs to draw from it a continuation of sounds, for which reason it is seldom heard except among the inhabitants of the mountains: the Hindoos of the flat country are too weak and of too delicate a frame to make use of such an instrument. The sound of the *Ramsinga,* is strong and rather agreeable when heard at a distance. There are Faquirs who play on it tolerably well.

In the higher Hindoostan the *Ramsinga* serves to open and close the great markets. The musicians who are sometimes heard with this instrument in the villages are sure to attract a great crowd.

Commentary

Sukumar Sen's *Etymological Dictionary of Bengali* derives the name "rāmśiṅgā" from *rām,* Bengali for "big" and *śiṅgā,* "horn", as an animal's horn, from which the instrument was originally made.[2] It is today most widely known as narsīgā or raṇsīga vaik, Hindi for "crooked war-horn". Das Gupta, in *Aspects of Bengali Society,* writes that the rāṅśiṅgā was used in ancient times by commanders to

RĀMŚIṄGĀ. Paris II.12.2.

issue directions to troops in the battlefield.[3]

According to Lalmani Misra, the instrument is fashioned from either copper or brass and produces two tones the interval of a fifth apart.[4] The S-shaped horn is most common in Himachal Pradesh and Bihar. It is played in Bihar in combination with the śahnāī and drums, such as the ḍhāk and ḍholki at weddings and in martial dances.[5]

NOTES

1 Babiracki and Helffer, "Narsīgā", NGMI, 2: 749. Variants: narsīghā, narsiṅga, narsinghā, and Solvyns's Bengali rāmśiṅgā.
2 803
3 83.
4 108.
5 Babiracki and Helffer, "Narsīgā", NGMI, 2: 749.

34. Bā̃k[1]

Calcutta: Sec. XI, No. 23. A Baunk, or Trumpet.
Paris: II.12.3. Baunck.

The *Baunck* may be very well compared to our trumpet both for the form and the sound. As it is common among the Hindoos that almost every body plays it, they endeavour to surpass each other, not in skill, but in noise: at their feasts the contest is whose *Baunck* shall be the loudest, and this strange rivality produces a confusion to which an European ear does not find it easy to get accustomed. The *Baunck* is painted red like the *Ramsinga.*

The middle distance of the drawing represents the habitation of a man of the country; it is built of earth and has a mat hung from a stick instead of a door. The master of the house is seated before this entrance; his costume is the dress of the cold season: farther on is another house of the same description: both of them are surrounded with cocoa-trees, bananas, mango-trees and palm-trees, with which all the country of Hindoostan is covered.

Commentary

This brass instrument appears not to enjoy the same popularity today as it did in the late eighteenth century. A similarly shaped end-blown trumpet is known as bānkīyā in Rajasthan. There it is played by the professional musician Sargura caste at marriages and other festive occasions.[2] In southern Bihar, the term *bā̃k* is applied to an S-shaped trumpet by the Oraon tribal people.[3]

Shoberl notes that it was used in processions and was employed by the Mārāṭhas as a military instrument for both cavalry and infantry.[4]

BÃK. Paris II.12.3.

NOTES

1 "Bā̃k", NGMI, 1: 112. Variant: bānk.
2 Dournon, "Bankiya", NGMI, 1: 155. Also see Kothari, 44, and Blowmik, 141.
3 "Bā̃k", NGMI, 1: 112.
4 3: 25.

35. Surnāī[1]

Calcutta: Sec. XI, No. 22. A Soorna, or Hautboy.
Paris: II.12.4. Soorna.

The *Soorna* is our hautboy; but the Hindoos play it so ill, that they can draw from it only shrill and disagreeable sounds; the European the most accustomed to the stunning of Hindoo music cannot stand a concert of several *Soornas* accompanied with some of their other noisy instruments. Every *Soorna* exerts his whole strength and entirely after his own fancy, without any respect to measure or harmony: at a distance one would imagine that it was the roaring of a number of wild beasts. The musician whom I have represented is before his house, and not in a very easy attitude.

The *Soorna* players are men of bad morals, and pass the greater part of the day in the shops of the retailers of *toddy* [*tāṛī*] and other spirits. There they recite at great length to those who will listen to them, the very shameful adventures of their lives, without omitting the most trifling circumstances of their gluttony and debauchery, with an exact amount of all the feasts where they assisted, and the quantity of victuals and of betel which they received.

Commentary

This is the double reed oboe-type aerophone common throughout Asia, the Middle East, and part of Africa affected by Islamic influence. The surnāī of Indian folk traditions differs from the classical śahnāī in that it includes a metal lip-disc, allowing the entire reed to be placed inside the mouth, while the reed of the śahnāī is lip-held.

SURNĀĪ. Paris II.12.4.

Both Risley and Bhattacharya refer to low caste Mucīs and Muslims who play drums and surnāī together in bands at weddings and festive occasions. "Those who play on the kettledrum and the pipe called *sanai*, and who are generally Mahomedans, are perched on the top of the main entrance. . . ."[2]

NOTES

1 Dick, "Surnāī", NGMI, 3: 478. Variant: surnāy. Also see Flora, "Śahnāī", NGMI, 3: 283-84. Variants: sanāī, shahnāī, shehnāī.

2 Bhattacharya, 213. Also see Risley, 2: 99.

36. Tobrie[1]

Calcutta: Sec. XI, No. 6. A Tobrie,—resembling the Bagpipe.
Paris: II.12.5. Tobrie.

The *Tobrie* is not unlike our bagpipe: they make this instrument out of a dried fruit hollowed out so as to admit three pipes of bambou, one above and two below, in which last there are several holes as in our clarinets; the performer blows into the upper pipe, and modifies the sound by stopping one or more of the holes in the lower ones.

The *Tobrie* is very common on the coast of Coromandel and in several provinces of Hindoostan: it is more rare upon the borders of the Ganges and of the Barampouter [Brahmaputra].

In the Carnatic, the Mauls [Māl],[2] or serpentmen, make use of the *Tobrie,* as they do of the Tomtom in the other provinces, to attract the serpents from their holes.

There is nevertheless nothing very enchanting in the sound of this instrument; the only thing in it which can give any pleasure to an European, is the expression which the Hindoos give to their sounds, and the variations which they take care to produce by the mixture of the *forte,* the *piano,* and the *crescendo.*

Commentary

The instrument described here is the common snake-charmer's pipe of India. The term Solvyns uses to designate the instrument is uncommon, and it is most widely known as the pūngī. In some parts of North India, this instrument is called tumbā, tumbī, or tomrā (all meaning "gourd"), and *An Etymological Dictionary of Bengali* gives *tumaṛi,* as the snake-charmers flute.[3] "Tobrie" might

TOBRIE. Paris II.12.5.

be a corruption of one of these. The instrument is made of a curved gourd about eighteen inches long, with an opening at the narrow end.[4]

Shoberl writes that "this instrument is played by barbers; it is used in all the pagodas, and likewise accompanies the dances of the *bayaderes* and *devedassees*".[5]

NOTES

1 Dick, "Pūngī", NGMI, 3:159. Variants: pū̃gi, puṅgī, poṅgā, poṅgi.
2 Solvyns portrays the Māl, I.11.4, without the tobrie, but in his etching of the Sāmperia ("Sauperea") snake-charmers, II.8.1, he depicts both the tobrie and huḍuk, an hourglass drum. The Māls are a cultivating caste among whom only a few "with gipsy habits" live by catching snakes. Risley, 2: 48.
3 Sukumar Sen, 405.
4 Bandyopadhyaya, 23.
5 3: 26.

37. Bā̃śi[1]

Calcutta: Sec. XI, No. 36. A Bunsee,—a Bomboo Flute as often played on through the nose as the mouth.
Paris: II.12.6. Bunsee.

The *Bunsee,* made of bambou, a very sonorous wood and consequently very fit for musical instruments, is the same as our common flute; but the Hindoos play it very differently, for, instead of putting it between their lips, they put it into their nose. Nothing is more comical than to see the flute merchants in the bazars surrounded by a group of amateurs with their flutes in their noses, trying the sound of the instruments with the most extraordinary grimaces. This strange custom has its origin in the religious opinion that a Hindoo of a superior cast is contaminated if his mouth should touch anything which has approached the mouth of an inferior. It is this scrupulous religious repugnance which makes them prefer playing the flute with their noses. It is sometimes carried to a very great excess: a woman of the lowest class thinks herself dishonoured, if a stranger should even see her mouth: when she meets one, her first care is to cover this part, though she should leave all the rest of her body exposed.

Commentary

The Bengali word for flute, *bā̃śi,* which Solvyns gives as "bunsee", is from the word for bamboo, *bā̃ś(a).* Originally of a particular species of bamboo, it was by the twentieth century more frequently of metal, wood, or ivory. Its length varies from about four to eighteen inches, with an opening to blow in, and six other

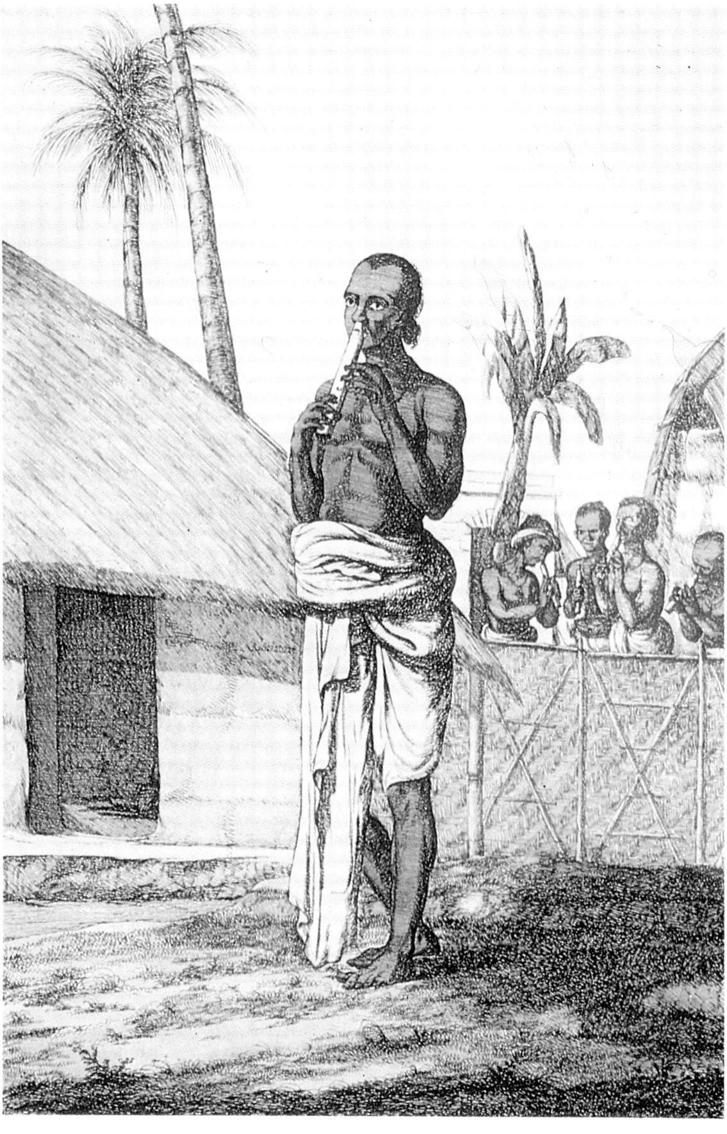

BÃŚI. Paris II.12.6.

openings for the fingers to play. In its association with Kṛṣṇa, it is usually known as muralī.[2]

C. R. Day writes that wind instruments are "looked upon as of secondary importance. Possibly this may have some reason in the fact that Brahmins are not allowed by their religious laws to use them, excepting only the flute blown by the nostrils, and one or two others of the horn or trumpet kind. And so men of low caste are employed as players of wind instruments".[3] Abbé J. A. Dubois, a contemporary of Solvyns in India, as we noted in the Introduction, also remarked on the pollution associated with wind instruments, the defilement arising from "the players contact by putting such instruments to their mouths after they have once been touched by saliva, . . . the one excretion from the human body for which Hindus display invincible horror".[4]

However, lip-blown transverse flutes are well-documented in ancient and medieval iconographic and textual sources in South Asia. End-blown flutes played by blowing air through the nose are not unknown in South Asia, but the transverse type seems to have been better known since antiquity, except during a period of decline during Muslim rule in North India, suggesting the possibility of a prohibition against the instrument by Muslim rulers because of its strong symbolic association with Kṛṣṇa, the divine cow-herd. Today, the end-blown flute is more commonly found in the westernmost parts of India, where it is known as the naṙ. The Indian nar is thought to be related to the Central and West Asian nāy.[5] The flute depicted here is apparently of the fipple type. Such instruments are most popular today among amateur players and folk musicians.

NOTES

1 Dournon and Helffer, "Bā̃suri", NGMI, 1: 192. Variants: bāṃsuri, bānsuri, bānsrī, bā̃srī, baṅgśi, bāśī, and, in Bengali, bā̃śi.

2 Das Gupta, 84; and Bandyopadhyaya, 20-22.

3 103.

4 64.

5 Dick, "Naṙ", NGMI, 2: 749.

38. Bhoraṅga[1]

Calcutta: Sec. XI, No. 29. A Burung,—used at the Hindoo Festivals.

COMMENTARY

The bhoraṅga (Solvyns's "Burung") is a long trumpet-like aerophone and seems to be what is most frequently known as the turya or turhī, with variants. The war trumpet of the *Mahābhārata* was the turya. In the Himalayan regions, the tubular karnal once signaled danger to neighbors across the hills, but today, as for all such horns, they are used, together with drums, principally for folk dance accompaniment. Each region of India has such a straight trumpet, and they are variously named.[2]

Shoberl, who follows Solvyns's text in the Paris edition for most of his descriptions, includes the instrument in his account of the music of Hindustan, but while Solvyns depicts the bhoraṅga in the Calcutta collection, it is omitted from the Paris edition. The instrument Shoberl depicts in his accompanying plate is very similar to Solvyns's "burung" and is described as "a long pipe called *tare* . . . , more particularly employed for the purpose of announcing the death of a person, or the offerings made by his relatives on his funeral pile. The dull, mournful tunes of this instrument render it very suitable for this office."[3]

Das Gupta, in *Aspects of Bengali Society,* describes the "bhoraṅg" as "a kind of pipe", consisting "of double tubes, one inner and the other outer. Clever manipulation of the instrument produced notes of different pitches. This is now practically out of use."[4] Such instruments, made from thin brass or copper sheets, produce what Bandyopadhyaya describes as a very harsh and loud sound that "cannot be considered to be musical, yet they were in great

BHORAṄGA. Calcutta XI.29.

use in bygone age in various ceremonial occasions of the Hindus, [blown at the beginning of functions] like religious festivals, marriage and in war."[5]

NOTES

1 Sukumar Sen, 727, lists bhoraṅga as "a kind of bugle", 727. Solvyns's contemporary in Bengal, the Rev. William Ward, 1: 259, refers to a "Bhorũngũ, a straight trumpet".

2 NGMI gives "turhī" as the "alternative term for the Narsĩgā of southern Bihar". 3: 682. Also see Deva, 111-12.

3 3: 24-25.

4 83.

5 23.

Bibliography

Note: Entries in *The New Grove Dictionary of Musical Instruments*, edited by Stanley Sadie, use the abbreviation NGMI.

Abu'l-Fazl 'Allāmī. *Ā'in-i-Akbarī* (Book III of *Akbar Nāma*, 1597). Translated by H. S. Jarrett, revised and annotated by Jadu-Nath Sarkar in "Sangīta", *Bibliotheca Indica*, Royal Asiatic Society of Bengal (Calcutta), 270 (1948).

Archer, Mildred. "Baltazard Solvyns and the Indian Picturesque", *The Connoisseur* 170 (January 1969): 12-18.

———. *Company Paintings: Indian Paintings of the British Period.* London: Victoria & Albert Museum, 1992.

———.*India and British Portraiture, 1770-1825.* London: Sotheby Park Bernet, 1979.

Archer, Mildred, and W. G. Archer. "Francois Baltazard Solvyns: Early Painter of Calcutta Life". In: *Science, Philosophy and Culture: Essays Presented in Honour of Humayun Kabir's Sixty-Second Birthday,* edited by Frank Moraes *et al,* 1-10. Bombay: Asia Publishing House, 1968.

Atanassov, Vergilij. "Daire". NGMI, 1: 536.

Babiracki, Carol M. "Karah". NGMI, 2: 360.

———. "Mădār". NGMI, 2: 590-91.

Babiracki, Carol M., and Mireille Helffer. "Narsīgā". NGMI, 2: 749.

Baily, John, and Alastair Dick. "Sārindā". NGMI, 3: 297-98.

Bandyopadhyaya, S. *Musical Instruments of India.* Varanasi: Chaukhambha Orientalia, 1980.

Bayly, C.A. *Indian Society and the Making of the British Empire.* New Cambridge History of India, II.1. Cambridge: Cambridge University Press, 1988.

Belnos, Mrs. S.C. *Twenty-Four Plates Illustrative of Hindoo and European Manners in Bengal.* Calcutta: Riddhi-India, 1979 [1832].

Bhattacharya, Jogendra Nath. *Hindu Castes and Sects.* Calcutta: Editions Indian, 1973 [1896].

Bird, William Hamilton. *The Oriental Miscellany: Being a Collection of the Most Favourite Airs of Hindoostan, Compiled and Adapted for the Harpsicord, & c.* Calcutta: Joph. Cooper, 1789.

Blowmik, S.K., ed. *The Heritage of Musical Instruments (A Catalogue of Musical Instruments in Museums of Gujarat).* Vadodara, Gujarat: Department of Museums, Government of Gujarat, 1990.

Bor, Joep. "The Rise of Ethnomusicology: Sources on Indian Music *c.* 1780-*c.*1890". *Yearbook for Traditional Music* 20 (1988): 51-73.

———. "The Voice of the Sarangi: An Illustrated History of Bowing in India". *National Centre for the Performing Arts Quarterly Journal* (Bombay) 15-16 (1986-87): 1-183.

Callcott, Lady (Maria). See Maria Graham.

Campbell, Capt. Donald. *Journey Over Land to India.* London: Cullen, 1795.

Capwell, Charles. *The Music of the Bauls of Bengal.* Kent, Ohio: Kent State University Press, 1986.

Carey, William. *A Dictionary of Bengal Language (Bengali-English).* 2 vols. New Delhi: Asian Educational Service, 1981 [1825].

Crooke, William. *Tribes and Castes of North Western India.* 4 vols. Delhi: Cosmo, 1974 [1896].

D'Alberg (Dalberg), Baron Johan Friedrich Hugo von. *Ueber die Musik der Indier Eine Ubhandlung des Sir William Jones.* Erfurt: Beyer und Maring, 1802.

Daniélou, Alain. *Hindu Polytheism.* New York: Pantheon, 1964.

Das Gupta, Tamonash C. *Aspects of Bengali Society from Old Bengali Literature.* Calcutta: Univesity of Calcutta, 1935.

Day, Charles R. *The Music and Musical Instruments of Southern India and the Deccan.* Delhi: B. R. Publishing Corp., 1974 [1891].

Della Valle, Pietro. *The Travels of Pietro Della Valle in India.* 2 vols. London: Haklvyt Society, 1892.

Deva, B. Chaitanya. *The Musical Instruments of India: Their History and Development.* Calcutta: Firma KLM, 1978.

Dick, Alastair. "Dendung",. NGMI, 1: 556.

———. "Ḍaph". NGMI, 1: 545-46.

———. "Esrāj". NGMI, 1: 719.

———. "Ghaḍasa". NGMI, 2: 39.

———. "Ghaṇṭā". NGMI, 2: 39-40

———. "Huḍukkā". NGMI, 2: 257-58.

———. "Kāṙā". NGMI, 3: 360.

———. "Kartāl". NGMI, 2: 361-62.

———. "Kā̃sar". NGMI, 2: 362.

———. "Khol". NGMI, 2: 423-24.

———. "Manjīrā", NGMI, 2: 609.
———. "Mṛdaṅga". NGMI, 2: 696-699.
———. "Naṛ". NGMI, 2: 749.
———. "Paṭaha". NGMI, 3: 21-22.
———. "Pinãk". NGMI, 3: 113.
———. "Pūngī". NGMI, 3: 159.
———. "Śaṅkh". NGMI, 3: 289-90.
———. "Sirbīṇ". NGMI, 3: 390
———. "Sitār".NGMI, 3: 392-400.
———. "Surmaṇḍal". NGMI, 3: 477.
———. "Surnāī". NGMI, 3: 478.
———. "Tambūrā". NGMI, 3: 514-15.
———. "Ṭikārā". NGMI, 3: 584.
Dick, Alastair, and Carol M. Babiracki. "Nagāṛā". NGMI, 2: 739-41.
Dick, Alastair, Carol M. Babiracki, and Geneviève Dournon. "Ḍhāk". NGMI, 1: 559.
Dick, Alastair, Carol M. Babiracki, and Mireille Helffer, "Ektār", NGMI, 1: 649-50.
Dick, Alastair, Carol M. Babiracki, and Natalie Webber. "Ḍholak". NGMI, 1: 562-63.
Dick, Alastair, and Geneviève Dournon. "Ḍhol". NGMI, 1: 560-62.
———. "Khanjari". NGMI, 2: 422.
Dick, Alastair, Gordon Geekie, and Richard Widdess. "Vīṇā". NGMI, 3: 728-35.
Dick, Alastair, and Devdan Sen. "Tablā". NGMI, 3: 492-97.
Dick, Alastair, and Neil Sorrell. "Rāvaṇhatthā". NGMI, 3: 198-99.
Dournon, Geneviève. "Bankiya". NGMI, 1: 155.
Dournon, Geneviève, and Mireille Helffer. "Bā̃suri". NGMI, 1: 192.
D'Oyly, Charles. *European in India.* London: Edward Orme, 1813.
Dubois, Abbé J. A. *Hindu Manners, Customs and Ceremonies,* 3rd edn. Oxford: Clarendon Press, 1959 [1816].
Dyson, Ketaki K. *A Various Universe: A Study of the Journals and Memoirs of British Men and Women in the Indian Subcontinent, 1765-1856.* Delhi: Oxford University Press, 1978.
Fenton, Mrs. E. *Journal of Mrs. Fenton—A Narrative of her life in India, the Isle of France (Mauritius), and Tasmania During the years 1826-1830.* Edited by H. W. Lawrence. London: Edward Arnold, 1901.
Flora, Reis. "Śhahnāī". NGMI, 3: 283-84.
Kothari, Komal. *Folk Musical Instruments of Rajasthan: A Folio.* Borunda: Rupayan Sansthan, Rajasthan Institute of Folklore, 1977.
Fowke, Francis. "'On the *Veena,* or *Indian* Lyre,' An Extract of a Letter from Francis Fowke, Esq. to the President". *Asiatick Researches.* New

Delhi: Cosmo, 1979 [1788], 1: 246-49. Reprinted with plate, in Tagore, 191-97.

French, Colonel P. T. "Catalogue of Indian Musical Instruments". In *Hindu Music from Various Authors,* edited by Sourindro Mohun Tagore. Chowkhamba Sanskrit Studies, 49. Varanasi: Chowkhamba Sanskrit Series Office, 1965 [1882] , 243-73.

Ghose, Nagendra Nath. *Memoirs of Maharaja Nubkissen Bahadur.* Calcutta: K. B. Basu, 1901.

Gold, Charles. *Oriental Drawings, Sketched Between 1791 and 1798.* London: G. & W. Nicoll, 1806.

Graham, Maria. *Letters on India* . London: Longman, 1814.

Hamilton, Walter. *A Description of Hindoostan.* Delhi: Oriental Publishers, 1971 [1820].

Hardgrave, Robert L., Jr. "A Portrait of Black Town: Baltazard Solvyns in Calcutta, 1791-1804". In *Changing Visions, Lasting Images: Calcutta Through 300 Years,* edited by Pratapaditya Pal, 31-46. Bombay: Marg, 1990.

———. *A Portrait of the Hindus: Baltazard Solvyns in Calcutta, 1791-1804.* Forthcoming.

Hardgrave, Robert L., Jr., and Stephen M. Slawek. "Instruments and Music Culture in Eighteenth Century India: The Solvyns Portraits". *Asian Music* 20 (Fall/Winter 1988-89): 1-92.

Heber, Reginald. *Narrative of a Journey Through the Upper Provinces of India, From Calcutta to Bombay, 1824-1825.* 2d edn. 3 vols. London: John Murray, 1828.

Hobson-Jobson. See Yule and Burnell.

Hood, Mantle. "Music, the Unknown". In *Musicology,* edited by Frank Harrison *et al.* 215-316. Englewood Cliffs, NJ: Prentice-Hall, 1963.

Ivie, G. I. Hamilton. *An Outline of Postal History and Practice, with a History of the Post Office in India.* Calcutta: 1910.

Jones, Sir William. "On the Musical Modes of the Hindus", *Asiatick Researches.* New Delhi: Cosmo, 1979 [1792], 3: 55-87. Reprinted in Tagore, 125-60.

———. "On the Gods of *Greece, Italy,* and *India*", *Asiatick Researches.* New Delhi: Cosmo, 1979 [1788], 1: 188-235.

Kencaid, Dennis. *British Social Life in India, 1608-1937.* London: George Routledge & Sons, 1938.

Kindersley, Mrs. Nathaniel. *Letters from the Island of Tenerisse, Brazil, the Cape of Good Hope, and the East Indies.* London: J. Nourse, 1777.

Kothari, Komal. *Folk Musical Instruments of Rajasthan: A Folio.* Borunda, India: Rupayan Sansthan, Rajasthan Institute of Folklore, 1977.

Kunst, Jaap. "Een Vergeten Musicologische Bron: De

Instrumentafbeeldingen in 'Les Hindous' Van F. Baltazard Solvyns". *Cultureel Indië.* Leiden. 7 (1945): 197-200.

Losty, J. P. *Calcutta: City of Palaces.* London: British Library/Arnold, 1990.

Martin, James Ranald. *Notes on the Medical Topography of Calcutta.* Calcutta: Bengal Military Orphen Press, 1837.

Meerwarth, A. M. *A Guide to the Collection of Musical Instruments Exhibited in the Ethnographic Gallery of the Indian Museum, Calcutta.* Calcutta: Zoological Survey of India, 1917.

Miner, Allyn. "The Sitar: An Overview of Change". *The World of Music* 32 (1990), 27-57.

———. *Sitar and Sarod in the 18th and 19th Centuries,* Intercultural Music Studies 5. Wilhelmshaven, Germany: Florian Noetzel Verlag, 1993.

Misra, Lalmani. *Bharatiya sangit vadya.* New Delhi: Bharatiya Jnanpith, 1973.

Mitra, Asok. *The Tribes and Castes of West Bengal,* Census 1951, West Bengal. Calcutta: West Bengal Government Press, 1953.

Nair, P. Thankappan, ed. *Calcutta in the 19th Century.* Calcutta: Firma KLM, 1989.

———, ed. *British Social Life in Ancient Calcutta (1750-1850).* Calcutta: Sanskrit Pustak Bhandar, 1983.

Nayak, Narendra Kumar, ed. *Calcutta 200 Years: A Tollygunge Club Perspective.* Calcutta: Tollygunge Club, 1981.

Nevile, Pran. "The Nautch Girl and the Sahib", *India Magazine* (January 1990): 42-52.

———. *Nautch Girls of India: Dancers, Singers, Playmates.* New Delhi: Ravi Kumar, 1996.

NGMI. See Sadie, Stanley. *The New Grove Dictionary of Musical Instruments.*

Nugent, Lady Maria. *A Journal From the Year 1811 till the Year 1815.* 2 vols. London: 1839.

Pal, Pratapaditya, and Vidya Dehejia. *From Merchants to Emperors: British Artists and India, 1757-1930.* Ithaca: Cornell University Press, 1986.

Parks, Fanny. *Wanderings of a Pilgrim, in Search of the Picturesque.* 2 vols. Karachi: Oxford University Press, 1975 [1850].

Pitoëss, Pribislav. "Timila". NGMI, 3: 586.

Ray, Sukumar. *Folk-Music of Eastern India, with Special Reference to Bengal.* Shimla: Indian Institute of Advanced Studies/Calcutta: Naya Prakash, 1988.

———. *Music of Eastern India.* Calcutta: Firma K. L. Mukhopadhyay, 1973.

Risley, Herbert H. *The Tribes and Castes of Bengal.* 2 vols. Calcutta: Bengal Secretariat Press, 1891.

Roberts, Emma. *Scenes and Characteristics of Hindostan.* 3 vols. London: W. H. Allen, 1835.

Sadie, Stanley, ed. *The New Grove Dictionary of Musical Instruments* [NGMI]. 3 vols. London: Macmillan, 1984.

Sanyal, Charu Chandra. *The Rajbansis of North Bengal.* The Asiatic Monograph Series, Vol. 11. Calcutta: The Asiatic Society, 1965.

Śārṅgadeva. *Saṅgitaratnākara.* Edited by Pandit S. Subrahmanya Sastri. Madras: The Adyar Library, 1951.

Sen, Prabhas. *Crafts of West Bengal.* Ahmedabad: Mapin, 1994.

Sen, Sukumar. *An Etymological Dictionary of Bengali: c. 1000-1800 A.D.* Calcutta: Eastern, 1971.

Shellim, Maurice. *India and the Daniells.* London: Inchcape/Spink & Co., 1979.

Sherring, Mathew A. *Hindu Tribes and Castes.* 3 vols. Delhi: Cosmo, 1974 [1872-1881].

Shoberl, Frederic, ed. *The World in Miniature: Hindoostan.* 6 vols. London: R. Ackermann [1822].

Shirali, Vishnudass. *Sargam: An Introduction to Indian Music.* New Delhi: Abhinav/Marg, 1977.

Sketches of India. London: Black, Parbury, and Allen, 1816.

Sonnerat, Pierre. *Voyage aux Indes Orientales et à la Chine.* 3 vols. Paris: L'auteur, 1782.

———. *A Voyage of the East-Indies and China,* trans. from the French, 3 vols. Calcutta: Stuart and Cooper, 1788, 1789.

Solvyns, François Baltazard. *A Catalogue of 250 Coloured Etchings; Descriptive of the Manners, Customs, Character, Dress, and Religious Ceremonies of the Hindoos.* Calcutta: Mirror Press, 1799.

———. *A Collection of Two Hundred and Fifty Coloured Etchings: Descriptive of the Manners, Customs and Dresses of the Hindoos.* Calcutta, 1796, 1799.

———. *The Costume of Indoostan* [pirated edition]. London: Edward Orme, 1804, 1807.

———. *Les Hindoûs.* 4 vols. Paris: Chez L'Auteur, 1808-1812.

Sorrell, Neil, and Mireille Helffer. "Sāraṅgī". NGMI, 3: 294-96.

Spear, Percival. *The Nabobs: A Study of the Social Life of the English in Eighteenth Century India.* London: Oxford University Press, 1963.

Tagore, Sourindro Mohun, ed., *Hindu Music From Various Authors,* Chowkhamba Sanskrit Studies, 49 (Varanasi: Chowkhamba Sanskrit Series Office, 1965 [1882].

Tennant, Rev. William. *Indian Recreation: consisting chiefly of strictures on the domestic and rural economy of the Mohomedans & Hindoos,* 2nd edn., 3 vols. London: Longman, Hurst, Rees & Orwe, 1804-08.

Yule, Henry, and A. C. Burnell. *Hobson-Jobson: A Glossary of Colloquial Anglo-Indian Words and Phrases.* 2nd edn., edited by William Crooke. Sittingbourne, Kent: Linguasia, 1994 [1886, 1903]. Notes identify the source as *Hobson-Jobson.*

Wallace, Lt. R. G. *Fifteen Years in India: Or Sketches of a Soldier's Life,* 2nd edn. London: Longman, Hurst, Rees, Orme, and Brown, 1823.

Ward, Rev. William. *A View of the History, Literature, and Mythology, of the Hindoos,* rev. edn., 3 vols. London: Black, Kingsbury, Parbury & Allen, 1822.

Welch, Stuart Cary. *Room for Wonder: Indian Painting during the British Period, 1760-1880.* New York: American Federation of Arts, 1978.

Whitworth, George C. *An Anglo-Indian Dictionary.* London: Kegan, Paul, Trench, 1885.

Willard, Capt. N. Augustus. "A Treatise on the Music of Hindoostan" (1834). In *Hindu Music from Various Authors,* edited by Sourindro Mohun Tagore. Chowkhamba Sanskrit Studies, 49. Varanasi: Chowkhamba Sanskrit Series Office, 1965 [1882], 1-122.

Wise, James. *Notes on the Races, Castes, and Trades of Eastern Bengal.* London: Harrison & Sons, 1883.